D1525813

ST. AUGUSTINE
ACADEMY PRESS

About Reverend P. Henry Matimore:

Patrick Henry Matimore was born in 1891 to Irish Immigrants in Chicago. After becoming a priest and receiving a doctorate in Sacred Theology, he briefly served as Superintendent of Schools for the Archdiocese of Chicago under Cardinal Mundelein from 1923-1926. By 1929, he was serving both as a professor of Education at Loyola University and as pastor of St. Clotilde's Church on the south side of Chicago. Despite his many duties, he still found time to produce a series of Catholic School Readers and to serve on the Advisory Board for the Journal of Religious Instruction. His parishioners affectionately remembered the good father strolling the neighborhood in the evenings with his dog "Rex," greeting all he met, especially the young people, for whom he always showed great concern. He retired in 1966, and died in 1972 at the age of 81.

About *A Child's Garden of Religion Stories:*

This first volume in the Madonna Series of study readers was intended for the third grade. Here we find stories from the early portions of the Old and New Testaments, beginning with Genesis and Exodus, and continuing through the Birth of Jesus to his early days of preaching. The volume closes with a selection of stories about the saints. In the second volume in the Madonna Series, *Wonder Stories of God's People*, the stories of the Old and New Testament are carried on with Jacob, Joseph, Samson and David, and the Miracles, Passion and Death of Our Lord, finishing once again with select stories of the saints. Then in the last of the three volumes, *Heroes of God's Church*, are found exclusively stories of the saints.

THE MADONNA SERIES
by
Rev. Patrick Henry Matimore
Former Superintendent of Schools for the Archdiocese of Chicago

This series of three study readers for the third through
fifth grade was originally produced in Chicago during the
reign of George Cardinal Mundelein in the early 1930s.
Each generously illustrated volume is based on stories from
the Bible and the Lives of the Saints.

A CHILD'S GARDEN OF RELIGION STORIES

A CHILD'S GARDEN OF RELIGION STORIES

By
REVEREND P. HENRY MATIMORE, S.T.D.

PROFESSOR OF EDUCATION, LOYOLA UNIVERSITY,
FORMERLY SUPERINTENDENT OF SCHOOLS IN
THE ARCHDIOCESE OF CHICAGO

ILLUSTRATED BY
CARL MICHEL BOOG

2018

ST. AUGUSTINE ACADEMY PRESS
HOMER GLEN, ILLINOIS

𝔑𝔦𝔥𝔦𝔩 𝔒𝔟𝔰𝔱𝔞𝔱:

    ARTHUR J. SCANLAN, S.T.D.,
      Censor Librorum.

𝔍𝔪𝔭𝔯𝔦𝔪𝔞𝔱𝔲𝔯:

    ✠ PATRICK CARDINAL HAYES,
      Archbishop of New York.

June 7, 1929.

This book was originally published in 1929 by The Macmillan Company. This facsimile edition reprinted in 2018 by St. Augustine Academy Press.

ISBN: 978-1-64051-071-5

To

HIS EMINENCE

GEORGE CARDINAL MUNDELEIN

FOREWORD

This is the first of a series of books that is offered to our Catholic schools as the fulfilment of a desire universally and constantly expressed by our Sisters for Catholic reading material. This volume is intended as a *real study reader*. Word and phrase difficulties are so arranged that their study must precede each story. The vocabulary is progressively difficult, but always within the actual or potential grasp of children of the Third Grade. A carefully planned Teachers' Manual suggests various ways of presenting the stories, but these suggestions are not designed to interfere with the originality of the teacher or the spontaneity of the class.

The author wishes to acknowledge a debt of the deepest gratitude to the Sisters and Community Supervisors who so graciously and capably assisted him in adapting these stories to the needs of our children.

CONTENTS

PART ONE

STORIES FROM THE OLD TESTAMENT

ix

PART TWO

STORIES FROM THE NEW TESTAMENT

PART THREE

HEROES IN GOD'S CHURCH

PART I

I

HOW GOD MADE THE WORLD

1. THE FIRST AND SECOND DAYS OF CREATION

This beautiful, big world in which we live did not always exist. But it is so very old that no one knows just exactly when it was made. There was a time when there was no golden sun nor silver moon nor twinkling stars. Indeed, long ago there was no earth at all. There was nothing but God. God always existed. He never had a beginning. He always was and always will be. We cannot imagine any time when God did not exist.

Then, thousands of years ago, God created heaven and earth. He made them from nothing. Only God can do this, because only He is all-powerful. But in the beginning, this wonderful world of ours was not as we see it to-day. There was a time when water covered everything, and all was darkness. And God said, "Be light made." And light was made. God called the light time *day* and the dark time *night*. This was the first day upon the earth.

On the second day, God made the clouds. He also made the beautiful blue sky as a home for the rolling white clouds. He called this *the heavens.*

2. THE THIRD, FOURTH, AND FIFTH DAYS

Then God said, "Let the waters that are under the heavens be gathered together in one place, and let the dry land appear." Such a rushing of waters that took place! Foamy waves almost as high as mountains dashed upon one another. Soon the great, deep oceans were formed. God called them *seas*. The dry land then rose up, and this He called the *earth*. As yet the earth was bare, so God said, "Let flowers, grass, bushes, and trees grow upon the earth." Then broad fields of waving grass, and bright-colored flowers, and fruit trees spread

over the earth.   When God looked at all these
pretty things, He saw that they were good.
These things He did on the third day.

The following day God made the sun, and
moon, and stars that we see in the sky. He
made these to divide the day from the night
for us.

After all these things were done, God created
the fish, and the animals that live in the sea,
and the birds that fly through the air. Fish
of all kinds, large and small, appeared in the

waters. Up and down, back and forth, they darted in the clear, pure water. Huge whales and sharks played in the deep, blue ocean. Trout, perch, and other small fish enjoyed the

cool waters of lakes and rivers. Birds of every form and color flew here and there among the trees. Merrily they chirped, and sang the sweet songs that God had taught them. This is what God did on the fifth day.

3. THE SIXTH DAY

On the sixth day God made the animals, big and little, wild and tame. The woods and fields began to live with beasts. In the forest could be seen the ivory tusks of large gray elephants, the brown, shaggy heads of lions, and the humps of clumsy camels. Indeed, God brought into the world cows, horses, goats, sheep, and every other kind of animal. Now there were birds in the air, fish in the sea, and beasts in the fields and forests. Pretty flowers, grass, and trees covered the land. What a wonderful world! But no man nor woman nor child was living in it yet.

God looked at all the things that He had made, and He was pleased with everything. But as yet He had not finished His work of creation. He wanted people to live in this lovely place. He said, "Let us make man to our image and likeness."

From such a common, useless thing as the dust of the earth, God made the body of the first man. Then into that body He breathed a soul that made it live — a soul that will never die. God called this first man Adam.

Thus man began to live in God's world. He could enjoy it and take care of it as no other creature could. Then, too, man could know who had made all these wonderful things, and, knowing God, he could love and serve Him. God made man master over every living creature.

4. THE SEVENTH DAY

After working for six days in making the world, God rested on the seventh day. He blessed this day and called it holy. God wants us to follow His example. He wants us to work for six days and then take a day for rest. We call our day of rest Sunday.

QUESTIONS

1. Has God always existed?
2. When did the world begin to exist?
3. Tell what God did on each of the six days of creation.
4. Why can you serve God better than the animals can?

II

THE GARDEN OF PARADISE

1. THE BEAUTIFUL GARDEN

God loved man more than all the other things that He had made. He wanted to please man and to give him a happy home. Therefore, as a sign of His love, He planted a beautiful garden, called the Garden of Paradise.

Here great oak trees, graceful elms, and tall poplars made shady lanes for man to walk in. Their leafy branches, swaying in the breeze, gave a home to the happy birds that filled the air with music. Fruit trees of every kind were bowed down to the earth with their rich burdens. What beautiful pears, apples, and oranges must have grown in God's garden!

Sweet-smelling flowers of red, pink, blue, and white were scattered over the grass. Cool, winding rivers gently flowed through the garden and watered everything that grew there. God

9

left nothing undone to make this the loveliest spot one could imagine.

Here God told Adam to make his home. How happy Adam was! How thankful to God

for His kindness! God gave Adam charge of the garden. Adam felt proud that God trusted him with this delightful place, and he loved to take care of all the things that were in it.

2. THE NAMING OF THE ANIMALS

Now, in the Garden of Paradise there were animals of every kind. Adam was often amazed at the difference among them. Some were long, others short. Some were tall, others small. Some were large, others tiny. Some were walking, some crawling, and others flying. The animals interested Adam, and every day he found out new and wonderful things about them.

One day God said to Adam: "It would be better if all these animals had names. Now, I am going to let you give them any name you wish. I shall bring them before you and they shall be known by the name you give them."

What a wonderful parade! There stood Adam in the garden, and before him passed a most interesting procession. Huge elephants with their wrinkled gray coats came swinging their trunks and flapping their long, flat ears. The long-necked giraffe could be seen far back in the line, his head towering above the others. Lions with shaggy manes marched side by side, and from time to time roared loudly to let Adam know that they were coming. Fierce-looking striped tigers walked along with timid, gentle sheep. Shining seals came flopping behind graceful deer. Animals, birds, and fishes of every kind appeared in turn before Adam

to receive their names. What a difficult task it must have been for Adam to give each a different name!

Probably Adam wanted to hear the voice of each of the animals so that he would know them by their voices. You can imagine what a choir they made with their roaring, screaming, singing, hooting, barking, baaing, shrieking, and howling.

3. GOD CREATES EVE

After Adam had given names to all the animals, he was tired. The shade of a large oak tree looked inviting, so he lay down to rest. He was thinking about all the animals that had passed before him. He said to himself: "It seems strange that all the animals that I saw to-day have companions of their own kind. There was not one that came alone. But here I am, master of this beautiful garden, and I have no one to talk to. How I wish I had a friend and companion!"

God knew that Adam had no companion — no man nor woman with whom he could talk. One day God said: "It is not well for man to be alone. Let us make him a helpmate like himself."

God then put Adam into a deep, deep sleep. We do not know just how long he slept, but while he was in this heavy slumber, God took one of his ribs and from it formed a woman. When Adam awoke, God brought the beautiful woman to him. He was very glad now because he had a friend and helpmate. He called her Eve. How they loved each other! They were very happy together in the garden that God had given them.

When twilight fell and the cool evening breeze rustled the leaves, Adam and Eve enjoyed rambling together along the winding paths. God often added to their pleasure by coming to walk and talk with them in the garden.

4. THE SERPENT TEMPTS EVE

For a long time, Adam and Eve lived in peace and happiness in their garden home. They were friendly with God and knew nothing wrong. God wanted them to prove their love for Him, so in the middle of the garden He planted a tree called the *tree of knowledge of good and evil*. One day He said to them: "Of every tree in the garden you may eat; but of the tree of knowledge of good and evil you shall not eat. For in whatsoever day you shall eat of it, you shall die the death."

Now, the devil took the form of a snake and came into the garden. He said to Eve, "Why did God command you not to eat of the fruit of every tree in the garden?"

"We may eat of the fruit of every tree except one," Eve answered. "God said that if we eat from that tree, we shall die."

Then the snake answered: "No, you will not die. But if you eat the fruit of that tree, you will be as God, knowing good from evil."

Eve listened to the snake. She gazed upon the tree. The longer she gazed, the more she desired to eat the forbidden fruit. Finally she thought that it would taste good and make her wise. So she put out her hand, picked some of the fruit, and ate it. Then she called Adam and gave him some.

5. GOD PUNISHES ADAM AND EVE

As soon as Adam and Eve had eaten the fruit, their hearts were filled with shame and fear. Now they were afraid to meet God; for they knew that they had done very wrong. So when they heard His voice in the garden, they hid among the trees.

Then God called to Adam, "Adam, where are you?"

Trembling with fear, Adam came to God and said: "Lord, I heard Your voice calling in the garden. I was afraid and hid myself."

"Why were you afraid to meet Me?" asked God. "You never hid from Me before. Have you eaten the forbidden fruit?"

Adam told the Lord that Eve gave him the fruit and he ate it.

Turning to the woman, God said, "What is this that you have done?"

"I ate it because the serpent lied to me," she replied with sorrow.

Then the Lord cursed the serpent and said that it should crawl in the dust and dirt forever. To Eve He said, "Because you have disobeyed Me, you will have sorrow and trouble all the days of your life." Then God looked at Adam and spoke these terrible words to him: "Because you listened to your wife and ate the fruit that I commanded you not to eat, the earth will be cursed in your work. With labor and toil you will earn your food until you die. For from the dust I made you, and into the dust you shall return."

6. OUT IN THE WILDERNESS

In His anger, God drove them out of the Garden of Paradise. They were indeed very sorry to leave the beautiful garden. Their only hope was that God promised to send some one to make up for their sin. With heavy hearts and saddened spirits, they went out of God's wonderful garden.   At the gate, God placed an angel with a flaming sword so that no one could enter again.

Out in the wilderness, Adam and Eve wept in sorrow.   God had been so good to them, and they had not been faithful to Him.   They had sinned against Him, and He had punished them. All the sorrow, misery, and suffering that is in the world to-day is the result of this sin of our first parents.   By this sin. Adam and Eve lost grace and stained their souls. And every child born into the world since then, except Mary, the Mother of God, has a stain upon his soul called *original sin.*

QUESTIONS

1. How did God show that He loved man better than His other creatures?
2. Can you describe the Garden of Paradise?
3. How did the animals get their names?
4. Why was Adam sad after he had named the animals?
5. Why did God forbid Adam and Eve to eat the fruit from the tree of knowledge?
6. What should Eve have done when the serpent first spoke to her?
7. How did God punish our first parents?
8. Did the sin of Adam and Eve have any effect on your life?

III

DRIFTING IN THE FLOOD

1. THE WICKED WORLD

In the beginning, when the world was still young, men lived much longer than they do to-day. Some lived to be eight or nine hundred years old. What a long time to live! When Adam died, he was more than nine hundred years old. God gave him many children. When these grew up, they married and had other children. Thus it was not so long before a great many people lived on the earth.

Some of these soon became wicked. As time went on, others followed their bad example, until almost everyone was wicked. They did not love God nor try to please Him. Their hearts were so bad that nearly all their actions were evil. They never thought of thanking God for all the good things He had given them. No song of praise to God was ever heard in their tents.

Even the little boys and girls were not trained to love and serve God. Mothers did not gather their little ones about them to tell them of the great God Who loved them. It was no wonder, then, that the children soon became as wicked as their parents.

God was very angry with these sinful people, for He had been kind to them, and had given them many blessings. They forgot all these things and lived as if God did not exist. God made up His mind to destroy them. He said that He was sorry that He had created man. He planned to punish the evil people by destroying them in a terrible flood.

2. THE FAITHFUL NOE

But when God looked upon the earth, He saw Noe, a good, honest man who loved and served Him. Noe was just, kind, and faithful. He tried to do what was right, although all about him were wicked. His sons also were trained to love and obey God. So God was pleased with Noe and sometimes talked with him.

Therefore, God did not want to destroy Noe and his family in the flood. He called Noe and told him of His plan to cover the earth with water. Every living thing would drown. But God said that He would reward Noe and his family for being good and would show them how to escape the flood. Noe was to build a large, strong boat, three stories high. Into the boat he was to bring his family, seven pairs of each of the animals used by man, and one pair of every other kind of animal. God also told him to store in the boat enough food to last his family and the animals about a year. We can imagine how large a boat was needed for the men, women, and children, the animals, and foodstuffs.

The pious Noe had faith in God. So with his sturdy sons, he began to build the boat that God called an *ark*. Trees in the neighboring forests were cut down and made into boards. For years and years, Noe's family worked on the ark. The wicked people often gathered to watch them. They made fun of Noe for building such a boat on dry land. But nothing could weaken Noe's faith nor his desire to obey God. Sometimes Noe tried to talk to the people about God and His punishment of sin, but they only laughed at him. He and his sons worked on, cheerfully and patiently. After years of labor, the boat was finished. There it stood on the land like a big house, with a large door near the bottom and a window near the top.

3. IN THE ARK

When God saw that everything was ready, He told Noe to bring his family and the animals into the ark. There was no sign of rain in the sky, but Noe obeyed. His sons and their families were the first to enter. Noe probably remained at the door to see that all the animals were safely in.

As far as Noe's eye could see, there was a long line of animals coming two by two. There were the brown giraffes with their long, slender necks, the prancing zebras with their striped backs, clumsy elephants with shining tusks, keen-eyed tigers, balky donkeys, and gentle cows. Tiny squirrels were there, too, and bob-tailed rabbits hopped along. In fact, Noe could count two of every kind of animal as they entered the great door of the ark. However, there were seven pairs of those animals that were very useful to

man, such as the cow and the sheep. When God saw that everything was in the ark according to His plans, He closed the door so that no other living thing could enter.

4. THE FLOOD

A few days passed, and rain began to fall. It rained as never before. It seemed as if the skies poured great floods of water upon the earth. Streams, rivers, and lakes began to overflow their banks. The frightened people fled from their homes in the beautiful valleys, and ran to the hills and mountains to escape drowning. Many

of them must have gone to the ark and begged Noe to let them enter. But they were doomed to disappointment.

The rain kept falling, and the water gradually crept up the hillsides. People climbed higher and higher on the hills, but the water continued to come closer and closer to them. Soon it covered the hills. Even those who had run to the top were drowned.

Those who had fled to the high mountains thought that they were safe. But God made the rain continue to fall after the hills were covered. So, little by little, the water crept up to the very tops of the mountains. For forty days and forty nights, the rain poured down in torrents, until every hill and mountain disappeared in the flood, and until every animal, bird, and man that was not in the ark was drowned.

How glad Noe and his family were that God had saved them! How thankful they must have been that He had told them to build the ark when they saw the terrible rain and heard its dull beat, beat, beat against the side of the boat.

When the waters had become deep enough, the ark began to float and drift. For six months it drifted in this direction and in that direction, and no one knew whither it was going. The boat had no sails, no rudder, no machinery. Therefore Noe could not direct its course.

It just kept drifting with the wind, and God made the wind blow so that the ark went where He wanted it to go. Finally it rested on the top of a mountain. Here it remained for two months. During this time the waters of the flood began to disappear gradually.

5. NOE'S MESSENGERS

Noe and his family became restless. It was very tiresome to be locked up in a boat for such a long time. Imagine how you would have disliked to be in it! Noe was eager to see if the land was dry, so he opened the window near the roof. He let a raven fly out. With its strong wings, this black bird flew away over the waters. But it did not come back to the ark.

A few days later, Noe sent out a dove; but this gentle bird could find no place to land, so it returned to the ark. After a week, Noe sent the bird out again. Towards evening, it returned with a green twig in its mouth. This showed Noe that the water must have gone down a great deal, because the trees were above the water.

The hearts of all in the ark beat with joy, for they knew that soon they would leave it. But Noe waited another week before he sent the dove out again. She flew away this time and

never returned. This was a sign, thought Noe, that the land was dry, and that it was time for them to leave the ark.

God spoke to Noe, and told him to bring his family and the animals out of the ark. The door was opened, and shouting with joy, Noe and his family stepped on dry land. The animals scampered hither and thither in their glee.

The birds chirped cheerfully and sang sweet songs as they flew from tree to tree. The sun, the green grass, and the trees seemed to Noe more beautiful than ever before.

6. GOD'S PROMISE TO NOE

Noe and his family were very thankful to the Lord for saving them when all others had died.

To show his thanks, Noe built an altar of stone. On this altar he killed and offered to God some of the animals which had been with him in the ark. This act we call *sacrifice*. When God saw how grateful they were to Him, he blessed them and took away the curse from the ground. Do you remember when God cursed the ground? It was after the sin of Adam and Eve. God promised Noe and his family that He would never again send another flood to drown the world. And to recall that promise to Noe and those who came after him, God placed a beautiful, colored rainbow in the sky. Whenever we see the rainbow in the sky, we should think of Noe and the flood.

COPY AND FILL IN THE BLANKS

1. God was very angry with the —— people because He had given them many ——.
2. God decided to save —— from the flood, because he was a —— man.
3. The boat which Noe built was called the ——.
4. Rain fell for —— days.
5. Noe first sent out a —— to see if the waters had gone down.
6. We should think of Noe and the flood whenever we see the —— in the sky.

IV

GOD CHOOSES ABRAHAM

1. THE FAITHFUL ABRAHAM

After the flood, the number of people increased rapidly, and before long there were a great many in the world. Some were good, others were bad. Many lost their faith in the one true God who had saved Noe in the flood. Some worshiped idols, or gods made of stone or wood. Others worshiped the moon as god. It was among these that Abraham lived. His relatives were rulers of the people. They were considered rich because they had large herds of cattle and flocks of sheep.

God loved Abraham because he was true and faithful to him. But God knew that it was not good for Abraham to live with people who worshiped false gods. He wanted to separate him from the wicked men, so that his children and their children and their children's children

could be trained and guarded as God's chosen
family.

God therefore said to Abraham: "Go forth
out of your country, and from your relatives,
and out of your father's home, and come into
the land which I shall show you.   And I shall
make of you a great nation.   And I shall bless
you.   I shall bless them that bless you and
curse them that curse you.   In you shall all
the people of the earth be blessed."

2. ABRAHAM OBEYS THE CALL OF GOD

Abraham never doubted the Lord but obeyed
at once.   He did not understand all that God
had told him.   Perhaps he never dreamed that
God meant that the Saviour would be born from
his descendants.   Neither did he know the
country to which God was sending him.   But
he had strong faith and was not afraid to go
where God called him.

Abraham brought the good news to his wife
Sara and then to his adopted son Lot, the
child of his dead brother.   They also were glad

to obey the Lord. So Abraham, with his aged father, his wife, and Lot, started on the journey. They took with them their servants, their tents, their flocks of sheep and their cattle, and

anything else they owned. In those days there were no wagons, trains, nor automobiles. Everybody had to ride on a camel or donkey, or walk on foot.

Imagine what a sight that was — sheep, cows, donkeys, men, women, and children slowly marching across the hot desert land. During the heat of the day, the travelers usually rested under their large black tents. The journey was continued when the evening breezes cooled the land. With the mooing of the cows, the baaing of the sheep and goats, and the shouting of those in care of the animals, there was little quiet along the trip. Every now and then, the herdsmen would run out, cracking their whips and shouting at the sheep or cows that tried to stray away. On and on they went, across rivers, through fields, and over hills.

3. IN THE LAND OF PROMISE

The journey was too long and tiresome for the old father of Abraham, and at one of the stopping places he died. After his burial, the travelers again started on the road toward their new home. At last they came to the land of Chanaan, which was the land God had promised to Abraham.

"This is the land," God said, "that I will give you." Abraham was very thankful for

God's kindness to him. He built an altar and worshiped God.

Abraham looked into the valley and saw that people were already living there. He decided to have nothing to do with them. So he pitched his tents on the hillsides or in the open fields, wherever he could find grass and water for his sheep and cattle.

4. ABRAHAM'S GREEDY SON

When Lot, Abraham's adopted son, grew to be a man, Abraham gave him servants, sheep,

and cattle. The flocks and herds of both Abraham and Lot soon became very numerous, and it was not always easy to find grass and water for them. This often brought about quarrels between the servants of Abraham and the servants of Lot. Each wanted the best places for his master's cattle and sheep.

It grieved Abraham to see the men quarreling. Finally, one day he took Lot up a near-by hillside, and said: "Let there be no quarrel between you and me, nor between your servants and my servants; for we are relatives. Behold, the whole land is before you. Depart from me, I pray you. If you go to the left, I will take the right. If you choose the right hand, I will pass to the left."

How noble and generous Abraham was! God had given the whole land to him. If he had desired, he could have told Lot to leave the land.

Lot saw the rich, green fields below him near the city of Sodom. He saw the barren hillsides, too. So he said to Abraham, "I choose

the valley." He left the barren hillside for Abraham's sheep and cattle. As time passed, Lot moved closer and closer to the city, until finally he moved into the city itself.

QUESTIONS

1. Why did God choose Abraham?
2. Why did God command him to leave his home?
3. How did Abraham and his party travel?
4. What was the name of the land God had promised to Abraham?
5. What kind of a man was Lot? Why do you think so?

V

WHEN FIRE FELL FROM HEAVEN

1. THE GUESTS

It was midday. The sun was high in the sky. Its hot rays beat down upon the dry earth. The sheep were dozing in the shade of the large oak trees, because it was too warm for them to feed in the open fields. Abraham was resting before his tent when he saw three persons coming down the road toward him. They did not look the same as other men, and Abraham knew that they did not live in the near-by country. Soon he saw that one was the Lord and the other two were angels.

Abraham ran out to meet them. He bowed low and said: "Lord, if I have found favor in Your sight, pass not away from the home of Your servant. Rest here under the tree, while I get some water to wash Your feet and some food to help You on Your journey."

In those days, people did not wear shoes as we do to-day. They went with bare feet or with sandals. Sandals kept the stones from hurting the feet, but they did not keep off the dust and

dirt. So after a long walk, people took off their sandals and washed their feet.

Abraham had his wife make some bread or cakes, while a servant cooked a young calf. When all was ready, Abraham served his guests. While they ate, he stood near them under a tree. The Lord told Abraham that his wife Sara would soon have a son. This pleased

Abraham and Sara very much, because they had prayed many, many years for a son.

2. ABRAHAM PLEADS FOR SODOM

After the meal was finished, the three arose to continue their journey. The two angels walked on ahead and took the road to Sodom. Abraham walked a short distance with the Lord. God told him that He was going to destroy Sodom, and Gomorrha, another city near by, because the people were wicked.

Abraham thought of Lot, whom he dearly loved. He did not want Lot to be destroyed, so he pleaded with the Lord for the city. He said: "Will you destroy the just with the wicked? If there be fifty just men in the city, will they die too? Will you not spare the city for the sake of the fifty just?"

And the Lord promised to save the city if fifty just men could be found in it.

Abraham began to fear that there might be less than fifty. So he spoke again: "I know that I am but dust and ashes, but seeing that

I have once begun, I shall speak again. Will you destroy the city if you find forty-five just men in it?"

God answered, "I will not destroy the city if I find forty-five just men in it."

Still Abraham was troubled. He kept pleading, and each time he made the number smaller. Finally he said: "I ask you not to be angry with me, Lord, if I speak once more. What if ten just persons should be found there?"

God knew that it was Abraham's love that made him plead in this manner, so He promised not to destroy the city if ten just men were found in it. Then the Lord journeyed on, and Abraham returned to his tent.

3. THE ANGELS AT THE HOME OF LOT

The two angels who went to Sodom spent the night with Lot. When the wicked men of the town heard about the two visitors at Lot's house, they hurried there, for they intended to do harm to the strangers. Lot would not allow these cruel men to enter his home, so they tried to break down the door.   Lot went outside the door to quiet the noisy men, but they only cried out the louder, and insisted that Lot bring the visitors out to them.   But Lot knew that

they intended to kill the strangers, so he refused to bring his visitors out or to let the wicked men in his home.   In their anger, they rushed at the door.

The angels stood inside near the door and heard all that was going on.   They partly opened the door, reached out, and quickly pulled Lot inside.   Then God struck the wicked men blind. The blinded men now became furious in their rage and tried to destroy Lot's home, but their blindness prevented them.

4. THE ANGELS HURRY LOT FROM THE CITY

The angels told Lot that they had come to destroy the city because there were not ten just men to be found in it. They warned him to tell his relatives in the city to flee before the wrath of God fell upon it. Lot hurried to the homes of his sons-in-law and gave them warning, but they only laughed at him.

Early the next morning, the angels urged Lot to hasten from the city with his wife and two daughters. But they did not want to leave their beautiful home and their riches. It was very hard for them to make up their minds to obey the angels. The angels then took them by the hand and forced them to leave the city.

When they arrived outside the city, one of the angels said to Lot: "Save your life; look not back. Neither stay in the near-by country, but save yourself in the mountains."

Lot begged the angels to let them flee to the little town close by, because he could not climb the mountains. The angels granted his request, and told him to hurry on his way because they would begin to destroy Sodom as soon as he was safe in the town to which he was going.

5. FIRE FROM HEAVEN

Then what a downpour of fire fell from heaven! Blazing clouds, pillars of fire, leaping flames, and lightning were sent by God upon the wicked cities of Sodom and Gomorrha.

Bright red flames and masses of curling black smoke burst from the burning cities. Shrieking men and women ran wildly here and there, but there was no escape. Every man, woman, and child in the two cities died in that awful fire.

Now God had commanded Lot and his family not to look back at the flaming city. But his wife was too curious. She wanted to see what was going on. She disobeyed God and looked back. God punished her by turning her into a pillar of salt. There she stood upon the plains, a warning to all not to disobey the commands of God.

The next morning, Abraham left his large black tent and walked to the top of the hill. He gazed with sadness down into the valley. There he saw nothing but smoke and ashes. Nothing remained of those beautiful houses. God had blotted the wicked cities and their wicked people from the earth. The heart of Abraham was sad, but he knew how good and just God is. Abraham loved God above all things, and it grieved him to see so many wicked people turn away from the love of God.

Before long, Abraham again moved his tents and herds to better pasture lands. It was here that the word of God came true. In this lovely fertile country, a little son, Isaac, was born to Abraham and Sara.

READ THE PARAGRAPH THAT TELLS

1. How Abraham greeted his visitors.
2. Why Abraham did not want the Lord to destroy Sodom.
3. How the wicked men of Sodom acted toward the angels.
4. How God destroyed Sodom and Gomorrha.
5. How God punished a curious woman.

VI

ABRAHAM PROVES HIS LOVE

1. ABRAHAM OBEYS GOD'S COMMAND

For years and years, Abraham and Sara had prayed to God and asked Him to send them a little child. As we read in the last story, God listened to their prayers and finally promised them that a boy would be born to Sara. When the little Isaac came, the hearts of Abraham and Sara were filled with joy. As the child grew older, they loved him more and more.

Finally God wanted to test Abraham and see how much Abraham loved Him. So one day He said, "Abraham, take your only son, Isaac, whom you love, and offer him as a sacrifice upon one of the mountains."

This command was a terrible blow to Abraham. Only God knew how long Abraham had prayed for the birth of Isaac. And only God knew how much the father loved his son. Now

God ordered Abraham to kill this son. Then
he was to offer Isaac as a sacrifice upon the
altar by burning his body. Abraham had
often offered in this way a sheep or goat, who
was then called the *victim* of the sacrifice, but

now the victim was to be his own dearly loved
son. Abraham's love for the God Who made
the world was greater than his love for Isaac,
so he prepared to obey God's command.

He told two servants to get things ready
for a journey of three days. Wood and food
were packed upon a little donkey. Soon the

father, son, and two servants started toward the mountain of sacrifice. Whenever they sat. down to rest, Abraham would embrace Isaac, telling him how much he loved him. Often tears came into the old man's eyes, but he hid them from the boy. Through it all, he had faith in God, for he thought that God would bring Isaac back to life after the sacrifice.

In due time, they arrived near the mountain chosen by God for the sacrifice. Abraham told the servants to remain behind with the donkey while he and Isaac went ahead to pray. Then he placed the wood for the sacrifice on the shoulders of Isaac, while he carried a little pot of fire and a sword. Thus the two went on together.

2. THE SACRIFICE OF ISAAC

As they drew near the place of sacrifice, Isaac said to Abraham: "Father, behold we have fire and wood. What shall we offer to God as a victim in this sacrifice?"

At first the old man was so overcome that he

could not reply. Finally with an effort he said,
"God will find a victim, my son."

When they had reached the mountain top,
Abraham gathered stones and built an altar.

Then the wood was placed upon it. The father
embraced his only son and said to him: "My
son, almost all my life I prayed that God would
give me a son. You came to me in my old
age. You have brought joy into my life. I
love you more than all else on earth. I would

gladly give my life for you. But our great God, Who made you and me, has commanded me to offer you, my dearly beloved son, upon this altar. I love you, but I love more the God Who gave you to me. I must obey His wish."

Then Abraham bound the boy's hands and feet, and laid him upon the altar. He drew his sword from his belt and raised it toward heaven. As he lowered it, his hand began to tremble. Just as he was about to strike Isaac's neck, Abraham heard a loud voice calling: "Abraham, lay not your hand upon the boy; neither do anything to him. Now I know that you fear God and have not spared your only son for My sake."

3. SPARED BY GOD

The sword fell from Abraham's hand. In his joy, the father clasped his son to his breast and kissed him over and over again. How glad he was that God did not wish the death of the boy he so dearly loved! Tears of joy rolled down his face, as he untied the cords that bound his beloved Isaac.

But in all his joy, Abraham did not forget God. He wanted to offer a sacrifice of thanks. Looking around, he saw a ram which had been caught by its horns in the bushes behind him. With the help of Isaac, he brought the ram to the altar, and offered it as a sacrifice instead of Isaac.

A second time the angel of the Lord called from heaven to Abraham, saying: "Because you have not spared your only son for My sake, I will bless you. You will have so many descendants that no one will be able to count them. And through your descendants, all the nations of the earth shall be blessed, because you have obeyed My voice."

ARE THESE TRUE OR FALSE?

1. God wanted to test Abraham's love for Him.
2. Abraham loved Isaac more than he loved God.
3. Wood and food were packed for the journey.
4. Abraham killed Isaac.
5. Abraham offered a goat as a sacrifice of thanks.
6. An angel told Abraham that God would bless him.

VII

CHOOSING A WIFE

(A Play)

CHARACTERS

ELIEZER, *servant of Abraham*   REBECCA
HIS COMPANIONS   BATHUEL, *her father*
                                  LABAN, *her brother*

PROLOGUE

Abraham was now an old man. He knew that he did not have many more years to live. Often his thoughts turned to his son Isaac, who had grown to be a man. Abraham wished to see Isaac happily married, but he did not want him to marry any of the maidens in their part of the country, because these worshiped false gods.

One day Abraham called Eliezer, his chief servant, and ordered him to go to the city of Abraham's brother and bring back a wife for

Isaac.　He knew that the daughters in this place remained true to God.

SCENE I

A well outside the city of Nachor.　Eliezer, with his companions and his camels, resting.

ELIEZER

O Lord, the God of my master Abraham. meet me to-day, I beg You, and show kindness to my master.　Behold, I stand near the spring, and the fair daughters of the people of this city will come out to draw water.　Now, I shall ask the maidens for a drink.　Let the one who answers that she will give both me and my camels a drink be the one chosen for the wife of Isaac.

COMPANION

Behold the beautiful maidens coming to the well with their water jars!　How gracefully they carry them on their shoulders!

ELIEZER

Sh! Let me test this one who has just filled her jar. (*He approaches the well.*) Good day, fair maiden! I pray you to give me a little water from your jar to drink. I have journeyed from afar and I am very thirsty.

REBECCA

Drink, my friend, and I shall also draw water for your camels to drink.

(*Eliezer drinks from Rebecca's jar, and watches her as she fills the drinking place for his camels.*)

ELIEZER

Here are golden earrings, pretty maiden, and
fine bracelets for your arms. Tell me, whose
daughter are you?

REBECCA

I am a daughter of the tribe of Nachor. My
father is Bathuel, the grandson of Nachor.

ELIEZER

Blessed be the Lord God Who has guided
me into the house of my master's brother! Fair
maiden, is there any place in your father's house
for me to stay?

REBECCA

We have plenty of room for you, your companions, and your camels. I shall hurry home
and let my father know that you are coming.
He will be delighted to entertain you.

The homes of the men of Nachor are always
open to the tired traveler. No one was ever yet
turned from our tents without first enjoying our
food and a good rest. Farewell!

SCENE II

The home of Bathuel.

LABAN

Greetings, blessed of the Lord! Welcome to our home! Why stand you outside? I have prepared room for you and a place for your camels.

BATHUEL

You are most welcome to our house, friend. After your long journey, you must be hungry and tired. Come, your lunch is ready.

ELIEZER

Most gracious master, I shall not eat until I have given you my message.

LABAN

Speak, then, noble sir.

ELIEZER

I am the chief servant of the great Abraham.

BATHUEL

Abraham, my father's brother? God be praised! How is our uncle?

ELIEZER

The Lord has blessed my master in a most wonderful manner. His name is great among all the people of the land. Servants, sheep, oxen, camels, goats, silver, and gold he has in plenty.

LABAN

Blessed be our uncle Abraham!

ELIEZER

He is now about one hundred and forty years old. He looks well, but his heart is sad. His dear wife Sara died some time ago.

LABAN

We have heard a great deal about Sara in these parts. She must have been a very beautiful woman.

BATHUEL

But, friend, what brings you on this long journey?

ELIEZER

My master Abraham thinks that it is time for his son Isaac to marry. But he will not have him marry any of the daughters of Chanaan because they worship false gods.

BATHUEL

Indeed, the daughters of Nachor have always remained faithful to the one and true God.

ELIEZER

That is why I came here. Abraham made me promise that I would try to bring back with me a maiden of your tribe to be the wife of Isaac.

LABAN

The daughters of Nachor are many and beautiful. I am sure that you will find one who will be worthy to be the wife of Isaac.

ELIEZER

Yes, I have seen your beautiful maidens. To-day, I sat near the well and saw them come and go. But God showed me the one that is to be the wife of Isaac.

LABAN

And pray how did He show you? Tell us about it.

ELIEZER

When I arrived at the well, I prayed to our God to show me the maiden I had come for. It happened like this: I was to ask each girl for a drink as she came with her water pot to the well. The one who said that she would give both me and my camels a drink should be the one chosen by God as the wife of Isaac.

BATHUEL

How did your plan work out?

ELIEZER

No sooner had I finished my prayer than I saw your daughter Rebecca coming to draw water. When I asked her for a drink, she answered, "Drink, my friend, and I shall also draw water for your camels to drink." And later, when she told me that she was of the family of Nachor, I knew that God had directed me aright.

LABAN

Then God has chosen our Rebecca to be the wife of the great leader Isaac! What glory and honor has come to our tribe!

ELIEZER

May I take the maiden to my master?

LABAN

We bow to the pleasure of God. It shall be as He wishes.

BATHUEL

Behold Rebecca is before you. Take her and go your way. Let her be the wife of your master's son, as the Lord has shown.

ELIEZER

Here, Rebecca, are gifts of gold, jewels, and garments from my master. Laban, here is something for you, too. And this beautiful robe my master sent to your mother.

REBECCA

How rich and generous is my new master! (*Goes out.*)

BATHUEL

Let us celebrate this wonderful day with a feast!

ELIEZER

One request more. I should like to depart before the sun rises on the morrow.

BATHUEL

Oh! Be not in such a hurry. Let Rebecca stay with us for at least ten days more.

ELIEZER

I cannot remain so long, for the master awaits me anxiously.

LABAN

Let us call Rebecca and ask her wishes.

BATHUEL

Rebecca! Rebecca!

REBECCA

(*Coming in*) You called me, father. What do you wish?

BATHUEL

Will you go with this man now, Rebecca, or will you stay with us for ten days more?

REBECCA

I shall go now, father, if you do not object. I can have my clothes and my maidservant ready before the dawn.

BATHUEL

My loving daughter, may God bless you and protect you. May He guide your every step and keep harm and sorrow from your door.

EPILOGUE

Long before the sun had risen high, Eliezer had placed Rebecca and her maid upon his best camel, and happily started towards the home of Abraham and Isaac.

COPY AND FILL IN THE BLANKS

1. Eliezer was sent to find a wife for ——.
2. Laban was the brother of ——.
3. The daughters of Chanaan worshiped —— gods.
4. God chose —— to be the wife of Isaac.
5. Rebecca's brother was named ——.
6. Rebecca started for her new home, riding on the back of a ——.

VIII

MOSES IN THE BULRUSHES
(A Play)

CHARACTERS

MOTHER	A FRIEND
FATHER	PRINCESS
MARY, *their daughter*	FIRST MAID
AARON, *their son*	SECOND MAID

PROLOGUE

At one time, many of the descendants of Abraham were living in Egypt. God blessed His people in many ways, and they soon became very rich and powerful.

After a few hundred years, the rulers in Egypt were changed. The new kings did not like the *Hebrews*, as the descendants of Abraham were called. They were afraid of them. So one of the rulers made them slaves, and placed cruel masters to watch them. These masters stood over them all day with whips, and forced them to make bricks, and to build great houses for the people of Egypt. But this cruel treatment only made the Hebrews stronger and held them together better. The king then made a law that every baby boy must be killed as soon as he was born. The hero of our story was born shortly after this law was made.

SCENE I

Home of Moses' parents, near the river Nile.

MOTHER

I am afraid that we cannot hide our baby boy any longer. Every day the soldiers search the house. For three months now I have kept him from their swords. I fear they will get him.

FATHER

Oh, he is such a wonderful child. We must not lose him. Is there nothing that can be done?

MOTHER

No. His cries are now so loud at times that I fear the soldiers or spies will hear him. Then they will kill us all.

MARY

Oh, these cruel men! Why don't they let us alone? We do not bother them.

FATHER

I think the king is afraid that, if war comes, we shall help his enemies.

FRIEND

And he would be getting what he deserves! I work like a slave all day making bricks, with a harsh master ready to beat me if I rest a moment.

FATHER

And all day long, I must carry large stones for the new temple. If I try to rest, the whip is lashed across my back.

MOTHER

Indeed, yesterday your tunic was covered with blood from the beating.

AARON

Mother, the baby is crying again.

MOTHER

Hurry, Mary, and keep him quiet. The soldiers may pass by at any time.

FATHER

We must do something with him. What can be done?

MOTHER

I have been thinking of putting him in a basket near the edge of the river. Some one may come along and rescue him. If anyone sees how beautiful our baby is, he will save him.

FATHER

Let us prepare that basket in which we have kept our apples.

MOTHER

I have already done so. For a week I have planned this. See the tar I have put on the inside of the basket to keep the water out.

FRIEND

It is now early morning. This would be a good time to bring the basket to the river. No one would ever guess what you are carrying.

MARY

Let me carry it.

FATHER

No. It is too heavy. But perhaps you can do something else for your brother.

MARY

You know, father, that I would do anything for my sweet little baby brother.

FATHER

Very well, then. Hide in the tall bulrushes and watch to see who takes the basket.

MOTHER

Come, Mary, you and I will go alone. Nobody will see us.

FATHER

May the God of Abraham, Isaac, and Jacob guide your steps. (*Mary and her mother go out, carrying the basket in which Moses is sleeping.*) O God, protect my boy. Send to his rescue some kind-hearted person.

SCENE II

Mary and her mother carry the basket down to the water's edge. The mother kisses the babe and places the basket on a rock near the bulrushes.

MARY

O mother, hurry away. Here come the princess and her maids. They may see you. I'll hide here.

MOTHER

God save you, my son.

(*She goes out. Mary hides among the bulrushes, as the princess and her maids enter.*)

MARY

O dear God, don't let them kill my baby brother! Save him from our cruel masters.

PRINCESS

Maids, how smooth the river is to-day!

FIRST MAID

Yes, it is just like a sheet of glass.

SECOND MAID

How clear and pure the water looks!

PRINCESS

Listen! What is that sound?

FIRST MAID

Someone is crying.

SECOND MAID

It sounds like a baby's voice. Where is the sound coming from?

PRINCESS

I see a basket over there beyond the path. Bring it to me.

MAID

(*Opening basket*) Oh, what a beautiful baby!

PRINCESS

This is one of the babes of the Hebrews.

MARY

(*Coming from her hiding place*) O great and noble princess, shall I call a Hebrew woman to nurse the child?

PRINCESS

Yes, do.   What a sweet little baby!   I shall adopt him, and he shall be called my son.   I shall make him a great leader among our people. (*Mary goes out.*)

FIRST MAID

What will your father, the king, say?

PRINCESS

I have always had my way with him.

SECOND MAID

Here comes the girl with the nurse.   (*Mary returns with her mother.*)

PRINCESS

Can you nurse this child for me? I shall pay you well for your work.

MOTHER

It will be the greatest joy of my life. But what shall I do when the soldiers of your father come?

PRINCESS

Tell them not to touch the son of the king's daughter. His name will be Moses. Take him home and then care for him. Every month bring him to the king's palace, because I wish to see him.

MOTHER

I promise you that I shall raise him as if he were my own son.

PRINCESS

Farewell, then, till next month.

MOTHER

(*After princess and maids leave*) O God! How good You are! I am to raise my own son for the daughter of the king. Help me, O Lord, to teach him, and to train him to love and serve You above all things, and to help Your chosen people.

QUESTIONS

1. Where does the first part of this play take place?
2. How did the Egyptians treat the Hebrews?
3. Why did the king command that all baby boys should be killed?
4. How did Moses' mother prepare the basket so as to keep the water out?
5. How was Moses saved?
6. Whom did the princess choose as nurse for the baby Moses?

IX

THE VOICE IN THE BURNING BUSH

1. MOSES' LOVE FOR HIS PEOPLE

We do not know just how long the mother of Moses took care of him. During the years he spent with her, she taught him about the great God of the Hebrews and the wonderful promises He had made to His people. Moses learned these lessons so well that he never forgot them.

Finally the Princess sent for the boy Moses, saying that he must now make his home in the royal palace.

The learned priests of the temple were Moses' teachers. He studied very hard and became very wise. Everyone admired the adopted son of the Princess. His home in the palace was very happy, and he remained there for almost forty years.

Moses never forgot his people, and he resolved that he would do all he could to set them free. Several times he tried to talk to the Hebrews, but they would pay no attention to him. Because of his interest in them, the king became angry with him and was going to kill him. So Moses left Egypt and went into the land of Madian.

2. MOSES, THE SHEPHERD

At Madian, Moses met an old priest who placed him in charge of some of his sheep. So much did the old man admire Moses that he soon gave him one of his daughters in marriage. For love of his people, Moses gave up the riches and pleasures of the king's palace and lived, an unknown wanderer, on the hillsides of Madian. The rich clothes of the prince were set aside for the poor dress of a mountain shepherd.

For almost forty years, in summer and in winter, the faithful Moses took care of his father-in-law's sheep. Often, as he watched the sheep doze in the shade of the large trees, he thought of his people, the slaves in distant Egypt. He prayed that God might have pity on their suffering, and set them free from the rule of Pharao.

3. GOD SPEAKS TO MOSES

One day while Moses was tending the sheep on Mount Horeb, he noticed a burning bush. He went near it and was surprised to see that

the fire was not destroying the bush. He heard a voice from the bush calling, "Moses! Moses!" He was startled and looked around, but could see no one.

The voice spoke on: "Come not near. Take the shoes from your feet, for the place on which you stand is holy ground. I am the God of Abraham, Isaac, and Jacob." Moses now hid his face, because he dared not look at God. And the Lord said to him: "I have seen the suffering of my people in Egypt, and I have heard their cries. Knowing their sorrows, I am going to free them and bring them out of that land into a good land. I will send you to Pharao that you may lead my people out of Egypt."

Moses thought that he was not great enough to do this. So he said to God, "Who am I, O Lord, that I should do this?" God told him that he would help him. Then Moses asked, "What shall I say when the people ask me who sent me?"

"Tell them that the Lord God of Abraham, Isaac, and Jacob sent you," said the Lord. "After you have spoken to the people, go to Pharao. Tell him that the Hebrew people want to go into the wilderness to offer sacrifice to their God. At first he will not let you go, but after I show him My power, he will be glad to see you depart."

4. MOSES OBEYS

"The people will not believe that you sent me," Moses answered. Then God gave him the power of performing wonderful things, so that the people would believe him. Moses could now turn his staff into a snake and back again into a staff. He could make his hand as white as snow, like the hand of a leper, and then bring back its natural color. He could pour water on the ground and make it turn into blood.

But Moses still pleaded: "I am not a good talker. Some one else might do more good." But God assured him that He would teach him what to say. Moses continued to beg God to send some better and more able man. God did not like all this pleading on the part of Moses. God had chosen him, and he was the one to do the work. However, to please him, God told him that he could take his brother Aaron with him. Aaron could do the talking but Moses must tell him what to say.

This satisfied Moses.   He brought the sheep back to his father-in-law, and told him that he must return to Egypt.   The old man blessed Moses as he started on his homeward journey. On the way, Moses met Aaron and told him all the Lord had said.   Arriving in Egypt, they called together all the leaders of the people and gave them the message from God.   To make them believe, Moses used all the wonderful powers God had given him.   When the Hebrews saw the snake, the white hand, and the blood, they believed that God had really sent Moses to save them.

QUESTIONS

1. How was Moses' life at Madian different from his life in Egypt?
2. What would be the difference between a burning bush near your home and the bush that Moses saw?
3. From the story, can you show that Moses was not a proud man?
4. What did God do so that the people would believe Moses?
5. How was Aaron to help Moses?

X

THE TEN PLAGUES

1. THE FIRST ATTEMPT

Moses and Aaron convinced the Hebrews, or the Israelites, as they were also called, that they were sent by God to free them from slavery. Then they went before Pharao and said, "Our God has commanded us to go a three days' journey into the wilderness and offer sacrifice to Him." They knew that the king would not let them go if they told him what they really intended to do.

When Pharao heard them, his face became red with anger. He thought of the thousands of slaves who spent their lives making bricks and building temples for him. He did not want new ideas like this put into their heads by Moses and Aaron. "Who is your God," he said, "that I should obey him? I do not know your God, and your people cannot go. The trouble is that your people have not enough to do. I shall give them so much work that they will have no time to talk about going three days into the wilderness to offer sacrifice."

Aaron answered, "Our God will soon let you feel His power."

2. THE HEBREW BRICKMAKERS

At that time Pharao had many of his Hebrew slaves at work making bricks. They mixed soil with sand, water, and straw. The straw was to prevent the bricks from cracking. The mixture was stamped into a smooth paste and placed in a wooden form. It was left for a week in the sun to dry, and was then ready for building. These people did not bake their bricks in a fire as we do.

The slaves had always been given the straw they used, but now Pharao called those in charge of the Hebrews, and ordered them not to give the slaves any more straw for their bricks. He said each one must make as many bricks as before, but he must find his own straw.

The slaves now had to look through the fields for straw, and this took a great deal of time. At the end of the day, they were beaten if they had not made as many bricks as before. Many of them, therefore, blamed Moses for their new misery and asked God to punish him.

3. THE SERPENTS AND THE RIVER OF BLOOD

Moses was sad when he saw what had happened, so he said to God, "O God, my talk with Pharao has only brought more suffering on my poor people."

God had warned him that he would find the king a hard-hearted man; but He had promised Moses that in the end his work would succeed. He told him to go again with Aaron to Pharao and show him some of the wonderful things he could do. As they stood before Pharao, Aaron cast his rod upon the floor. At once it turned into a hissing serpent. Pharao called his wise men, and at the king's orders they likewise turned their rods into serpents. Then Aaron's serpent leaped upon those of the Egyptians and ate them. But the heart of Pharao was not changed and he paid no attention to the request of Moses and Aaron.

God now told Moses and Aaron to go to the river the next morning, where they would meet Pharao. "Tell him that you will turn the water into blood unless he lets your people go," said the Lord. They met the king at the river next day, and again asked him to let the Israelites go. The king refused. Then Aaron struck the water with his rod, and it turned into blood. Men could not drink the water, and all the

fish died. This lasted for seven days. Then God changed the blood back into water. But still the heart of Pharao was not moved.

4. THE FROGS AND BUGS

At God's command, Moses next said that he would fill the land with frogs unless Pharao changed his mind. The ruler did not think that this would really happen, so he still refused to let them go. Soon big frogs and little frogs were everywhere—in the fields, in the streets, and in the houses. He sent for Moses, and

begged him to drive the frogs back into the
water.   Moses agreed to do this if Pharao would
promise to let the people depart. Pharao
promised, and Moses asked God to chase the
frogs from the land.   But as soon as the king

saw the land free from frogs, he refused to let
the people go.

To punish Pharao, God now covered his king-
dom with lice, fleas, and flies.   But where the
Israelites lived, there were none of these insects.
Again Pharao sent for Moses, and pleaded with

him to send the insects away. He told him to have the Israelites offer their sacrifice in Egypt. But Moses reminded him that this would be impossible, because his people offered in their sacrifice cattle and sheep which the people of Egypt thought sacred. Pharao then said that they could go into the wilderness, but not any farther. Moses then asked God to remove the flies and bugs. No sooner were they gone than the king again refused to keep his word.

5. THE LAST PLAGUE

God sent plague after plague to Egypt. While the plague was in the land, Pharao would promise to allow the Israelites to depart; but as soon as it was removed, he refused to let them go. First, God sent a plague of sickness that killed thousands of cattle. Then followed a plague of sores and boils. Later, hail and rain poured from heaven. Then grasshoppers filled the land. This was followed by a plague of darkness. But none of these could change the stubborn heart of the proud king.

Finally God told Moses that the next blow would be final, and after it was struck, Pharao would order them from the land. God said that he would cause sorrow and woe to come into every home in Egypt, because He was going to kill the first-born of every man and beast in the kingdom, from Pharao down to the poorest in the land.

CAN YOU ANSWER THESE?

1. Why was Pharao so anxious to keep the Hebrew slaves in his country?
2. At first how did Pharao punish the Hebrews?
3. What made Pharao change his mind so often?
4. What forced Pharao to let the Israelites leave Egypt?

XI

THE FIRST FEAST OF THE PASSOVER

1. PHARAO REFUSES MOSES' LAST REQUEST

When God chooses some one to do a great work, He always helps him to do the work well. So it was with Moses. God called him to lead the Israelites out of Egypt, and promised to help him overcome the stubborn Pharao. Pharao was the most powerful king in the world, and he did not want to lose his Hebrew slaves. Nine times God sent terrible plagues over the land of Egypt to make Pharao free the Israelites. But his hard and cruel heart would not allow them to leave.

God was patient with Pharao, and He saved His greatest blow till the last. He sent Moses to Pharao to warn him that, unless he let the Israelites go, the oldest son of every family in his kingdom would die. This message angered the proud Pharao. He ordered Moses from his palace, and said he would kill him if he ever entered again.

The Lord then explained His plans to Moses. He said that in every Hebrew home, the master of the house must get a young lamb on the tenth day of the month. The lamb was to be killed on the fourteenth day. Its blood was to be sprinkled on the sides and at the top of the entrance to the house. In the evening it was to be roasted, and served with bread baked without yeast. Everyone in the house must eat it standing up and dressed as if ready for traveling. Nobody was to leave the house that night, because the angel of death would go through Egypt. But God promised that the angel would pass by the houses marked with the blood of the lamb.

2. THE LAST NIGHT IN EGYPT

Moses hurried to his people and told them all that the Lord had said. He ordered them to gather in families and tribes, and to make preparations for their departure. This was to take place on the morning following the last terrible blow with which God would strike the people of Egypt.

The poor slaves shouted with joy at the news. They sang the praises of God and His messenger,

Moses. It was the first time that they really showed any love toward their leader. They were all careful to do just as Moses told them. The evening of the fourteenth day found them all gathered about the table, eating the lamb whose blood stained their door posts. Imagine the prayers of thanks that rose that night from those happy hearts! God had not forgotten them in all their trials! He was now going to bring them into the land promised to Abraham, Isaac, and Jacob. Prayers of thanks, songs of praise, and stories of the former glory of their people filled the air. There was no sleep for the Israelites that night.

3. GOD'S LAST PLAGUE

In the middle of the night, the angel of death went through the land; he did not stop at houses where the door was stained with the blood of

the lamb. For the Hebrews, therefore, this feast was called the Feast of the Passover, because the angel of death *passed over* the homes of the Hebrews, and left the first-born in each free from harm. This day was sacred to the Hebrews, and they have kept its memory by celebrating the feast every year since.

But what cries and screams of despair came from the homes of the Egyptians! Into every home the angel of death entered, and killed the oldest son. Even in the palace, the proud Pharao's own son lay upon his bed cold in death. Now, indeed, Pharao felt the power of God. His eyes were opened, but it was too late to save his son. He had refused to listen to Moses and the commands of God, and his stubborn will brought death and sorrow all over the land.

In tears his people came to him, and begged him to let the Israelites go before their God should send further trials upon them. The Pharao saw that he could hold out no longer. He sent messengers to Moses and Aaron to command them to take the Israelites out of Egypt forever. It was only this terrible blow of death that changed his hard heart. He now feared God's power, and he was glad to see the Hebrews depart from his kingdom.

HOW

1. Did God show His patience with Pharao?
2. Was the angel of death to know the Hebrew homes?
3. Was the first Feast of the Passover eaten?
4. Did Pharao act after the death of the first-born?

XII

SLAVES NO LONGER

1. THE DEPARTURE FROM EGYPT

After the angel of death had killed the first-born in Egypt, Pharao commanded the Israelites to leave the country. This news spread quickly through the land. All things had been prepared, and the anxious people waited for Moses to give the order to depart. There were six hundred thousand men, women, and children gathered in tribes and families. What a throng of people! Tents, household articles, and other things were packed on donkeys and camels. The larger camels were used for carrying the children and some of the women.

Imagine that wonderful sight! Thousands and thousands of people with thousands and thousands of sheep, donkeys, cows, and camels! God and His angels must have smiled from heaven at the happy hearts of His chosen people.

He had freed them from the hand of Pharao.
Now He was leading them toward the Land of
Promise and was Himself going before them on
the journey.   In awe and wonder, the Israelites
followed their guide.   At night it was like a

flaming pillar, reaching far into the sky.   During the day, it was a long, narrow mass of
slowly-moving clouds.

How good God was to His chosen people
to lead them in this wonderful way into the
land He had promised them!   No longer did
any doubts or fears fill their minds.   They knew

that God was with them, and it did not matter who was against them.

During the journey, the Lord was always thoughtful of His people. When they became weary or tired, the pillar of cloud or fire stood still. Then the Israelites pitched their tents, ate their meals, and rested. When they were ready to travel again, the pillar moved before them.

On and on they went, through the desert, and over hills and plains. At last, they arrived at the shore of the Red Sea. Here they set up their tents for the night.

2. PURSUED BY PHARAO

To their horror, they looked behind and saw the army of Pharao on the top of a distant hill. Pharao was angry with himself for letting his useful Hebrew slaves depart. He gathered his soldiers and chariots together and rushed after the Israelites to bring them back. When he saw them in the camp near the Red Sea, he was delighted. He thought that he would have no difficulty in capturing them and forcing them to return.

Nearer and nearer came the tramp, tramp, tramp of the soldiers' feet and the din of Pharao's rumbling chariot wheels. Each shout of the approaching soldiers made the hearts of the Israelites tremble. They almost gave up in despair. They saw the waters of the Red Sea before them and the swords of Pharao behind them. They thought that there was no escape. Death in the wilderness! Death by the sword of Pharao! Death in the waters of the sea! Loudly they raised their voices against Moses. They cursed the day that he led them from Egypt. To these terrified people, a life of slavery was better than death at the hands of the angry Pharao.

But Moses never lost faith in the Lord. Standing before the excited people, he calmed them with these words: "Fear not. Stand and see the great wonders of the Lord, which He will do this day. For the Egyptians, whom you see now, you shall see no more forever. The

Lord will fight for you; and you shall hold your peace."

3. CROSSING THE RED SEA

The cloud that had led the Israelites to the sea now went behind them. Like a great wall,

it stood between them and the soldiers of Pharao. The side of the cloud that faced Pharao was so darkened that he could not see his former slaves. But the side that was turned toward the followers of Moses lit up their camp.

God then told Moses to stretch his hand over

the sea. When Moses did this, there arose a strong, burning wind that blew all night. In the morning, the excited Israelites saw a dry path through the sea to the other shore. Moses commanded them to march to the other side.

There was no need for a second command. No one had to urge them on. As fast as they could go, men, women, children, sheep, cattle, and camels hastened through the path that God had made. The waters on both sides formed two large walls, but the people did not fear the water nearly as much as they feared the soldiers of Pharao that were behind them. They knew that God had again shown his power and delivered them from the swords of the Egyptians. A few hours before, they were facing despair and death when they thought they were about to be captured by the cruel Pharao. Then their suffering in Egypt seemed to have been useless, but now they knew that God's loving care would bring them safe into the long-desired Land of Promise.

4. THE DROWNING OF PHARAO'S ARMY

When they had arrived safely on the other shore, the Lord lifted the cloud that hid the Israelites from the view of the Egyptians. Pharao was enraged when he saw that his former slaves had escaped through the dry path in the sea. He urged his chariots and soldiers onward. They dashed after the disappearing Israelites. Into the dried path, with the sea on both sides, they ran, shouting at the fleeing slaves.

But when the last of the Israelites had reached the shore, and the Egyptians were hurrying along the path, Moses again raised his hand over the sea. The angry waters dashed together and filled up the dry path.

The chariots stuck in the mud and the powerful horses struggled to pull them to land. Time

and again their heads rose in the foamy waves, but there was no hope. Riders tried to urge their horses on in their fight with death, but their efforts, too, were of no use. Horses and riders were drowned at the bottom of the sea. It was thus that God saved His chosen people.

ARE THESE TRUE OR FALSE?

1. Pharao commanded the Egyptians to leave the country.

2. When the Israelites seemed weary or tired, the pillar of cloud kept moving onward.

3. Pharao was glad he had let the Israelites go.

4. Moses never lost faith in' the Lord.

5. The waters of the Red Sea drew back to allow the Israelites to cross over.

6. God saved the Egyptian horses and riders from drowning.

XIII

AN UNGRATEFUL PEOPLE

1. COMPLAINING AGAIN

The miracle which God worked to enable the Israelites to cross the Red Sea in safety proved the greatness of His love for them. In their joy, they offered sacrifices of thanksgiving, and sang songs praising the power and the glory of God. The sister of Moses and other women went from tent to tent, dancing and singing. They sang the song that Moses had written to celebrate this happy event. This famous song begins: "Let us sing to the Lord, for He is gloriously praised. The horse and his rider He has thrown into the sea."

In a wonderful manner, God had saved them, and dashed their enemies to death in the angry waves of the sea. Surely we might expect that they would never again complain against God, nor forget His kindness to them. But we shall see how soon God's favors and kindness were forgotten.

Leaving the shores of the Red Sea, Moses led his people through the wilderness over desert lands and rocky soil. Traveling was not pleasant. Their sandals did not protect the feet of the pilgrims from the sharp rocks. The hot rays of the desert sun beat upon them without mercy. The food supply was fast giving out. Murmurs and complaints against Moses and Aaron were whispered, as the tribes and families gathered in their tents. Here and there the leaders of the tribes openly spoke against Moses. They said that they and their flocks were dying of thirst.

Moses did not like to hear them complain so much. He pleaded with them to be patient and to trust in God. But the Israelites forgot about God. They had faith when He showered them with favors, but when trials came they soon forgot the favors. In spite of Moses' good example and pleadings, the people continued to murmur against their leader and their God.

2. THE BITTER WATER

For a few days, God permitted this ungrateful people to suffer from lack of water. Then one hot day, when the complaining was at its worst,

loud cries of "Water! Water!" arose from those who had gone hunting for a well or spring. They had found a spring some distance ahead. The news spread like a fire alarm from tent to tent. Everybody took up the cry, "Water! Water!" Children rushed from the tents, old men and women hobbled along with canes, and all the others hurried to the water.

Eagerly they stooped down to drink, quarreling and pushing to see who should drink first. But alas! those who tasted the water, spit it out. Others tried, but followed the example of the first who drank. Those standing at some distance who were clamoring for a drink became angry when the first ones spit the water out. But soon they had their turn, and did likewise. The water was bitter as gall.

How this angered the Israelites! Louder and louder they cried out against Moses. Oh, why had they ever left Egypt? Slavery was better than death in the desert.

Moses became alarmed. He prayed to God to help him.

God told Moses to cut down a certain tree, and cast it into the water. When the Israelites saw Moses with ax in hand, chopping the tree, they made fun of him. Moses now paid little attention to their ridicule. Presently, he cast the tree into the water, and told the people to drink.

But they merely jeered at him. What a foolish idea to think that a tree would turn bitter water sweet!

So Moses and his brother Aaron filled jugs with the water, and drank and drank. The people thought this strange. A few near by tasted the water again, and found it pure and sweet. Others soon followed their example. When everybody had taken enough, the flocks and herds were led out to drink. Then water bags of skin were filled for future use.

What queer bags these were! A large piece of the skin of a cow or a deer was carefully cleaned on the inside. The corners were then gathered together and held while the water was poured in. Then the corners were tightly bound to form a neck for the skin bottle. We often see pictures of donkeys carrying several of these bags. Men going on long journeys sometimes tied them to their belt.

The water satisfied the Israelites for only a short time. On and on through the desert, they continued their way. Before long, however, the discontented people began again to murmur their old complaints. Life in Egypt as slaves rather than death from starvation! Life in Egypt rather than death in the wilderness! Their grain supply had given out. Milk and dates became their daily food, and they soon grew tired of them. Milk and dates morning, noon, and night did not make a very pleasant diet. Oh, how these poor people regretted having left the land of slavery!

3. GOD FEEDS HIS PEOPLE

The strong faith of Moses never doubted. He knew that God would help His people, so he prayed for food. God loved Moses and listened to his prayer. And with all their faults, He loved the Israelites too. He told Moses that his followers would have meat that night and bread the next day.

When twilight began to darken the land, great flocks of brown birds called *quail* flew above the camp. Lower and lower they flew. In and out over the tents they darted, as if to say, "Shoot us! Shoot us!" The Israelites ran from their tents, and gazed in awe at the wonderful sight. Never before had they seen anything like it. The men were so taken by surprise that they

forgot their hunger, and never thought of shooting the birds. But the boys hurried for their bows and arrows, and soon bird after bird fell to the ground. The action of the boys brought the men to their senses. Some used bows and arrows, others used slings with stones. As fast as the birds fell, the little children gathered them into piles. What excitement! What joy for the boys and girls! This was God's gift that made everyone happy. That night, the delicious odor of roasting quail went up from every camp fire.

Everybody feasted on quail. Peals of laughter and songs of joy rang out from every tent. When the feasting and singing ended, a happy and contented people lay down to rest upon their hard beds. In those early days, beds such as we have to-day were unknown. People slept upon mats made from straw and skins of animals, which were thrown on the ground. How different from our soft mattresses and springs!

4. MANNA FROM HEAVEN

The following day, when the sun had scattered the darkness of night, the Israelites arose. When the early risers came out of the tents, for a moment they gazed in speechless amazement at what they saw. The earth, the tops of the tents, the trees were covered with little white flakes like snow. Soon their cries of wonder aroused the whole camp. Eyes fresh from sleep blinked at the snowy white sheet that covered the earth. "What is it? What is it?" cried everyone. No one but Moses could answer that question.

Moses must have enjoyed the surprise of the people. When they saw him smiling calmly at

their excitement, they rushed to him asking, "What is it? What is it?" He told them that this was the food God had promised them. Each day, he said, they were to gather enough for the meals of one day only. However, on the sixth day of the week, they were to gather enough for two days because God would not send the food on the seventh. The Israelites could cook the food in any way they wished. Some greedy men thought that they would store some of the food away. But after the first day, it rotted and spoiled. Others did not obey Moses, and on the sixth day did not gather enough for two days. These found that they had none for the seventh day, because God did not send any on that day. Thus God taught them to obey the words of Moses.

The Israelites spent forty years in the desert, and during all those years God gave them this bread from heaven. They called it *manna* because when they first saw it, every one cried out "Manna" which means, "What is it?"

5. THE BREAD OF EVERLASTING LIFE

Hundreds and hundreds of years later, Our Lord Jesus Christ spoke to the Jews about this bread. He was telling the people about the food that He was soon to give them. He said to them: "I am the Bread of life. Your fathers did eat manna in the desert and are dead. I am the living Bread that came down from heaven. If any man eat of this Bread, he shall live forever; and the Bread that I will give is My Flesh, for the life of the world."

In this sermon, Our Lord compared the manna that God sent to the Israelites in the desert with His own Body and Blood that is received in Holy Communion. He told the Jews that the manna which their forefathers ate in the desert was only a food for the body. It did not have any effect on the soul. It did not bring grace to the soul. Those who ate it did not become more holy. But the Bread that He promised was different. It was His own real Body and Blood that was to be received in Holy Communion. To those who receive Communion worthily, He promised everlasting life with God in heaven. Then, too, He said that those who do not receive Holy Communion cannot expect to have His grace and blessing.

Our Bread from heaven, moreover, is greater than the manna in the desert because it is God Himself.

SEE HOW MUCH YOU KNOW

1. Why is the story called *An Ungrateful People?*
2. Make a list of five things that God did for the Israelites for which they should have been thankful.
3. How did God punish those who were greedy?
4. How was manna like Holy Communion?
5. How did Our Lord say it was different?

XIV

CAMPING IN THE VALLEY

1. WATER FROM THE ROCK

Shortly after God began to give the Israelites manna for food, He told them to continue their

journey through the wilderness. They took down their tents, after they had untied the ropes and lowered the poles. Then the men packed the tents, bed-mats, clothes, food, and other household articles. These they carefully fastened on the backs of camels. The women of the tribes gathered together and wondered what the future would bring. As usual, the small children and many of the women rode on camels and donkeys.

Sometimes they traveled through desert land, sometimes over large stretches of rolling prairies. Here and there, a lonely, silent tree may have given shady rest to the weary pilgrims. On and on they went for days until they reached a valley. Here Moses commanded them to halt.

In a few hours, the appearance of the place was entirely changed. There below the hill, a whole city was soon built. Great tents without number covered the ground. The entire place became a moving mass of life, with men, women, children, camels, cows, sheep, and goats going in this direction and that.

After fixing the tents, some of the men went out in search of water. They had had little water for several days. Up and down the land, they looked for wells or springs. Others tried to dig wells. But no water could be found. The pitiful cry of children begging for water made the Israelites sad. Women became weak from thirst. So once more the crowd was angry with Moses. They mocked him and jeered at him, saying that he had brought them out of Egypt to kill them by thirst. They grew to hate him more and more. Some even plotted to kill him.

Their anger filled Moses with fear. He knew how good and kind God had been to them. Day after day, they had been given manna to eat, and still they were not satisfied. What an ungrateful people! They were happy when they had everything they wanted to eat and drink; but when trials or sufferings came, they were always ready to grumble against Moses and God.

Moses now pleaded with God to send them water. God told him to strike with his rod a rock on the mountain side, and water would pour forth. Moses gathered some of the leaders of the people about him, and struck the rock with his rod. Splash! With a gush and a roar, the water burst from the mountain. Down it dashed, leaping and jumping over the rocks! It was a torrent of splashing foam. How fast it moved into the valley below, passing the tents of the Israelites! As soon as the cry, "Water! Water!" filled the camp, there was a wild rush

for the sparkling stream. Men, women, and children knelt on the ground and drank the foaming water or filled their skin bags with it. Once more the Israelites had faith in Moses. They cheered and praised him as the great leader sent to them by God. But Moses was disgusted with the folly of this wicked people.

2. THE FIRST BATTLE

It was in this place that the Israelites had their first experience of war. The people who had long been living at the other end of the valley did not like the idea of these strangers coming into their land. Amalec, their leader, gathered together his men, armed them for war, and marched toward the Israelites.

When Moses saw the approaching army, he ordered Josue to command the army of Israel. The brave and fearless Josue quickly selected his soldiers. Into the valley he dashed and attacked the forces of Amalec.

Moses stood with Aaron and Hur on the top of a hill to see the battle. Backwards and forwards, the armies pushed their way. Now they plunged forward in anger, now they ran backward in fear! Victory seemed to swing between them. First it was on the side of Amalec, then on the side of Josue. Sometimes Moses and Aaron would tremble with fear when the forces of Israel were on the run. Then suddenly the soldiers of Josue would gain courage, turn around, dash upon the enemy, and put them to flight. Again, Amalec would inspire new life in his men, and they would return the attack with vigor.

Whenever Moses raised his hand that held his famous rod, the army of Josue gained courage and drove the enemy back. Moses, however, could not keep his hands up all the time. It was a tiresome task. So he sat down on a rock while Aaron and Hur held up his hands for him. Josue from now on was master of the field, and finally succeeded in driving the entire army of the enemy out of the valley in defeat.

QUESTIONS

1. Which part of this story do you like best?
2. Why was Moses disgusted with the folly of the Israelites?
3. Did God take care of the bodily needs of His people?
4. Who commanded the army of the Israelites?
5. How did Moses help his people to win the battle?

XV

THE TEN COMMANDMENTS

1. MOUNT SINAI

About three months after the Israelites had fled from Egypt, they pitched their tents at the foot of Mount Sinai. This was a great stone mountain that rose sharply from the plains. Moses climbed the mountain to speak with God. God told him to say to the Israelites that if they would obey Him, He would make them His chosen people.

Moses gave this message to the people. "We shall do all that the Lord desires," they replied. God then told Moses to have the people prepare themselves to meet Him in three days.

At the dawn of the third day, the Israelites were awakened by loud, rolling peals of thunder and sharp flashes of lightning. Their hearts trembled with fear. What a sight they saw! The whole of Mount Sinai was covered with heavy, black smoke, curling and tossing in all directions. It looked as if the whole mountain was a burning furnace. Then from the top of

the mountain came the sound of a trumpet. It was a piercing blast that grew louder and longer.

Was it any wonder, then, that the faces of the men turned pale while their hearts trembled in fear? Could we blame the women and children if in terror they hid themselves in the tents?

Indeed, we can easily imagine the scenes in the tents with crying children clinging to frightened mothers. Moses spoke to the alarmed people, and told them that God would not harm them.

2. GOD ANNOUNCES HIS COMMANDMENTS

Presently, between the peals of thunder, the flashes of lightning, and the blasts of the trumpet, the voice of the Lord was heard loud and clear. The Lord announced to the trembling people, His ten great laws or *commandments:*

1. I am the Lord thy God. Thou shalt not have strange gods before Me.
2. Thou shalt not take the name of the Lord thy God in vain.
3. Remember thou keep holy the Sabbath day.
4. Honor thy father and thy mother.
5. Thou shalt not kill.
6. Thou shalt not commit adultery.
7. Thou shalt not steal.
8. Thou shalt not bear false witness against thy neighbor.

9. Thou shalt not covet thy neighbor's wife.

10. Thou shalt not covet thy neighbor's goods.

This was a terrible experience for the followers of Moses. In their fright, they withdrew a little from the foot of the mountain. The majesty of God's voice calling forth His commandments made them tremble. In their fear and terror, they looked to Moses for protection from the hand of God. They were willing now to follow Moses as their leader, and obey his wishes. "You are God's messenger to us," they cried out. "Tell us what God wants us to do and we shall do it. Let not the Lord speak to us again, lest we die."

Moses stood before them and told them that there was no need of being afraid. "God," he said, "has come to test you and to fill your hearts with a holy fear that you may sin no more." Indeed their hearts were filled with fear, and they promised never again to offend God by sin. But their fear soon passed away, and before very long they forgot their promises.

COPY AND FILL THESE BLANKS

1. The Israelites pitched their tents at ——.
2. They replied to the message of Moses ——.
3. The Israelites were awakened by ——.
4. The Ten Commandments were given to the Israelites by ——.
5. The majesty of God's voice made the Israelites ——.

XVI

THE GOLDEN CALF

1. MOSES SPEAKS WITH GOD

Shortly after God gave His commandments on top of Mount Sinai, He told Moses to go up the mountain. Josue went part of the way with Moses, but remained on the mountain side while Moses went to the top. There, for forty days and forty nights, the leader of the Israelites spoke with God. God explained many things to him. He told Moses how He wanted the people to worship Him; how to build the tent which was to serve as a church, and how to decorate it; how the priests should dress; and how to make Aaron high priest. In fact, God told him all about the divine services.

Don't you think that Moses must have been very happy during those forty days? And don't you think that he must have listened eagerly to every word that fell from the lips of God?

But during those forty days, the Israelites in the valley became restless. They wondered what had happened to Moses. For weeks and weeks they had not seen him. Some probably thought that he was dead and that they were left in the great wilderness without a leader. Discontent spread rapidly. How much longer must they wait to hear from Moses? Oh! why did they ever leave Egypt?

2. THE ISRAELITES ASK FOR IDOLS

They grew more and more impatient. They wanted to move on. Finally, they decided to wait no longer. They gathered before Aaron and said: "Arise! Make us gods that may go before us. For as to this Moses, the man that brought us out of the land of Egypt, we know not what has befallen him."

What a bold request! They stood before the future high priest of the Lord and demanded that he make them an idol to worship. They had seen the statues of cows that the Egyptians worshiped. Now they wanted to have the same.

Just a few weeks before, they had trembled at the voice of God calling out the commandments. In fear and awe, they had heard Him say, "I am the Lord, Thy God. Thou shalt not have strange gods before Me. Thou shalt not make to thyself the image of anything that is in heaven above or on the earth beneath. Thou shalt not adore them nor serve them."

They had made a holy promise to Moses to keep the law of God. They had said that they would do anything that God commanded. And now, after a few short weeks, they asked Aaron to make them an image of a cow that they might adore it.

3. AARON, THE WEAK LEADER

In the absence of Moses, Aaron was the leader. What a poor leader he made! He knew what an awful crime it was to worship an idol. Did he try to save the people from this terrible sin? Did he remind them of the visit of the true God to their camp just a few weeks before? Did he tell them of the presence of God on the mountain even then? Did he recall for them the wonderful things that God had done for them? No, he did none of these things. Perhaps he was afraid that they would kill him.

"Take the gold earrings from the ears of your wives and your sons and daughters, and bring them to me," he said to those who asked for the idol. The Israelites were delighted. The men hurried through the camp, gathering the gold from the people. In their joy, they placed several baskets filled with gold before the tent of Aaron. A fire was soon built, and a large pot holding the gold was placed over it. When the gold was melted, Aaron placed it in a mold and formed it in the shape of a calf.

Out into the middle of the camp, the Israelites carried their golden calf-god. High upon an altar it was placed. Bowing low before it, they cried out, "These are thy gods, O Israel, that have brought thee out of the land of Egypt."

When Aaron saw how pleased the Israelites were with their calf-god, he built an altar for sacrifice before it. He then sent a messenger through the camp to tell the people that the feast of the Lord would be celebrated the next day. What a celebration! God's chosen people offered sacrifices to a golden calf and worshiped

it as god! They bowed low in adoration. They sang and danced around the idol as they had seen the Egyptians do.

4. GOD'S ANGER IS ROUSED

Now, while all this was going on in the valley, God was talking to Moses on the mountain top. His all-seeing eye saw the wicked people adoring the golden calf. Their actions filled Him with anger. Just a few weeks before, they had promised to serve and obey Him alone as the one and only true God. Now they worshiped the image of a calf as god.

God decided to destroy this unfaithful people. He said to Moses, "Go down to the camp. The people that you brought out of the land of Egypt have sinned. They have wandered from the way you showed them. They have made a golden calf, and have adored it, saying, 'This is your god, O Israel, which brought you out of the land of Egypt.' I shall destroy this ungrateful people. But I shall make a great nation of your family."

Moses loved the Israelites, even though they did little to deserve his love. So he pleaded with God to spare them. Time and again, during the past months, Moses had prayed to God for his people. Time and again, God had listened to his prayer. And now, once more the prayer of Moses saved the forgetful people. God promised not to destroy the Israelites for their sin.

5. MOSES HASTENS TO THE CAMP

Moses now started down the mountain side. He, too, was angry with his people. In his hands he carried two large stone tablets on which God had written His commandments. The excited Moses hurriedly descended the stony footpath. Halfway down the mountain, he met Josue, his faithful friend. Moses told him what God had said about the Israelites.

Josue soon heard the shouting of the people. He turned to Moses, saying, "The noise of battle is heard in the camp."

Moses listened. He, too, heard the sound of voices. But his keen ear told him that it was not the cry of men urging soldiers on to fight. Neither was it the shout of victors chasing the enemy. "I hear the voice of singers," he said.

On reaching one of the open spaces at the foot of the mountain, they saw the camp. Both stood still for a moment. What was going on? What could all this mean? Men, women, and children were singing and dancing around the middle of the camp. Moses saw that they were bowing before the altar of the golden calf.

His eyes flashed with rage. From the top of Sinai, he had carried down the tables on which

God had written His law. But what was the use of giving these people the law of God? In his anger, Moses dashed the stones upon a rock. The law of God, written by God's own hand, was smashed into pieces. Josue trembled as the bits of stone scattered on the ground.

6. THE RETURN OF THE LEADER

The angry Moses hastened into the camp. When the Israelites saw him coming, they stopped singing and dancing before the idol.

Many ran to their tents, while others silently disappeared. He rushed up to the idol and dashed it to the ground. Bit by bit, he smashed it into fine powder. This he cast into the water that the Israelites had to drink.

What a change in the camp! A few hours before, the wicked people were singing and dancing before the golden calf. Now the idol was destroyed, and they were facing their angry leader. We can easily imagine how sternly he must have scolded them.

Moses was especially enraged with his brother Aaron. He knew that Aaron was to be the high priest of God. And it was this Aaron who had made the false god for the people to worship. It was Aaron who had really led them into their sin. How ashamed Aaron must have felt when Moses destroyed his idol! The thought of running from the camp surely must have entered his mind. But Moses had seen him, and he could not escape. Moses gave him a look filled with disgust. "What has this people done to you," he said, "that you should bring upon them a terrible sin?"

Aaron was a coward. He tried to place all the blame on the Israelites. In an effort to excuse himself, he said, "Do not be angry. You know that this people is inclined to evil. They asked me to make them a god. So I only did what they wanted when I made the golden calf."

7. THE CHOICE

Aaron's answer only made Moses more angry still. He withdrew a short distance from the crowd, near the gate of the camp, and cried out, "If any man be on the Lord's side, let him join with me." Now was the time for them to make their choice. Now they could choose between a statue of gold and the Lord God of the world. Surely it was a simple choice! There should have been no room for doubt. But some of the Israelites did doubt. Some turned away. Others hesitated. It was only the sons of the tribe of Levi that passed to the side of Moses.

Moses then ordered these faithful ones to take their swords and go through the camp, killing all those who still wished to worship the golden calf. Twenty-three thousand were killed that day.

CAN YOU TELL

1. Why the Israelites asked Aaron to make them a golden calf?

2. Why the sin of Aaron was greater than the sin of the people?

3. Why Moses was a stronger and better leader than Aaron?

4. Why the sin of worshiping the calf was especially terrible for the Israelites?

5. How Moses punished the wicked people?

XVII

SO NEAR AND YET SO FAR

1. BREAKING CAMP

The days of wandering through the wilderness were fast drawing to a close. Loud blasts sounded from silver trumpets and echoed through the camp. It was the sign for which the Israelites were waiting. It meant that they were to break camp and go forward to the Promised Land. Cheers and shouts of joy went up from every tent. For almost a year the Israelites had lived under the shadows of Mount Sinai. Now they were to continue their journey to the land that God had promised to the children of Abraham, Isaac, and Jacob.

It did not take the happy people long to pull down their tents and pack their baggage on the camels. Moses had commanded them to march in tribes. The tribe of Juda took the lead. Close behind followed the tribe of Issachar.

Then the others joined in order. The sons of Dan were in the rear.

What a wonderful parade! Thousands and thousands of men, women, and children, with their herds of cattle and flocks of sheep! Camels with shaggy brown hair — some laden with tents, others carrying women and children! Shepherds with long staffs, running here and there driving back the wandering cattle and sheep!

2. THE PILLAR OF CLOUD AND FIRE

God was still the leader of that large throng of people. He went before them by day in a pillar of cloud, and by night in a pillar of fire. At the head of the tribes was carried the Ark of the Covenant. This was a large box, made of precious wood and covered with gold on the inside and out. Two beautiful, golden angels were placed on the top. Inside the box were the two stones on which God had written His law. In one of the other stories we read that Moses broke the stone tables that God had given him. But later God commanded him to make two other tablets, and on these God again wrote His commandments. God told Moses to put these stones, together with some of the manna, in the Ark of the Covenant.

The pillar of cloud and fire showed the Israelites that God was with them. He was their guide and helper. There was no need to fear and surely no reason to complain. But they did grumble and complain. Don't you think that they were a very ungrateful people? First they cried for water, and then for meat. It seemed that they would never be satisfied. God punished them now. Some He killed with fire, others died with sickness.

3. THE SPIES

After some days of travel, the Israelites pitched their tents at Pharan. They were now near the Promised Land. Their days of journeying through the hot desert seemed about to come to an end. The land of their dreams was close at hand. God told Moses to send men ahead to look over the Promised Land. One from each tribe was selected. Moses ordered them to go out and see the famous place, and to learn all they could about it. They were to notice if the ground was fertile. They were to watch for the men who lived there, and see if they looked to be strong or weak. They were to see if the cities were protected with high walls.

These men were called *spies*, because they were to spy or find out all about the Land of Promise. For forty days, they went about their work, climbing hills and crossing valleys. Such a beautiful land! Large spreading shade trees and trees loaded with delicious fruits were found in great numbers. But the spies did not like the kind of men that dwelt there. They feared them, for they were like giants. The large high walls around the cities also helped to fill the hearts of the men with bitter disappointment.

After forty days, they returned to their camp, carrying different kinds of fruit that grew in the Promised Land. Moses and the Israelites were delighted when they saw such wonderful fruit. They thought that in a few days they would be living in the rich land.

But their joy was turned to bitter sorrow after they heard the report of the spies. "The land, indeed, is very rich in fruits of all kinds," said those who had been sent ahead, "but the people who live there are large and strong. They looked like giants. We seemed like grasshoppers beside them. Then, too, their cities have high walls around them. There is no hope. We cannot fight these terrible men." The Israelites cried out in rage when they heard all this.

Caleb and Josue, two of the spies, did not agree with the others. They tried to calm the people. The brave and fearless Caleb stood before them and said, "Let us go up and take the land, for we shall be able to conquer it."

But the others who had been with him answered, "No, we cannot go up to this people, because they are stronger than we are."

The Israelites believed the words of the cowards — the timid spies who were afraid to fight. Josue tried to urge the crowd to trust in God Who had guided them thus far, but they jeered and hooted him.

4. THE DISAPPOINTED ISRAELITES

The whole camp was so disappointed that almost everyone spent the night in tears. Men sobbed and women wept. They thought that all was lost. Here they were, just on the border of the Promised Land, and they could not enter it! The long-looked-for prize was within their grasp, and still it was not to be theirs. They repeated their old cry about Egypt, "Why, oh, why did we ever leave Egypt?"

The following day, some of the leaders of the tribes gathered together. They said to one another, "Let us appoint a captain, and let us return into Egypt." This sad news soon reached the ears of Moses and Aaron. They pitied the poor people, and their hearts were filled with sorrow. However, they thought that it would be useless to argue at the time, so they fell down flat upon the ground before the Israelites.

Josue and Caleb did not like to see the people turn against Moses. They knew that Moses was doing the will of God. Josue tried to change the spirit of the Israelites. He spoke to them about the wonderful things in the Land of Promise. He begged them not to rebel against God. He said that there was no reason to fear the people who lived in the desired land. "The Lord is with us," he said. "Fear not."

His bravery had no effect on the discouraged people. It only increased their anger. They picked up stones to kill both Caleb and Josue.

But at this moment the glory of God appeared at the ark. The stern voice of God was heard saying to Moses: "How long will this people despise Me? How long will they refuse to believe, after all the things that I have done for them? I shall strike them with sickness and they will die."

It was the loyal Moses that again saved his people. Only a short time before they had wanted to reject him. They had intended to kill his friends. But Moses forgave them all, and once more asked God to pardon them. "Forgive, I pray You," he said, "the sins of this people according to the greatness of Your mercy.

Do not let the Egyptians say that the God of Israel was not strong enough to keep His promise. They will say that You killed the Israelites in the desert because You could not bring them into the Promised Land. Be patient with them and have mercy on them."

5. GOD PUNISHES HIS PEOPLE

God answered the prayer of Moses, and said that He would forgive the Israelites, but He would punish them. He said that not an Israelite over twenty years of age would see the Promised Land, except Caleb and Josue. The others would live and die in the desert, and for forty years they would wander in the wilderness.

When the people heard the message of God, they were filled with shame and sorrow. The next morning, many of the chief men in the tribes came before Moses and said that they were ready to go into the Promised Land. Moses told them that they had come too late. They must now obey the command of God and return into the desert.

But the men refused to obey Moses. With their swords they started towards the people who lived in the Promised Land. When these saw the Israelites approaching like soldiers ready for battle, the leaders called their men to arms. They soon dashed upon the Israelites. When the followers of Moses saw the advancing army, they knew that the battle was lost. In through the disordered ranks of Israel, the sturdy soldiers of the enemy dashed, striking with swords to the right and the left. Man after man of the Israelites fell to the ground dead. Many fled. The enemy followed close behind, driving them into the camp itself. They had disobeyed God's wish. Death and disgrace were their punishment.

REVIEW

Tell one thing you know about each of the following persons:

1. Lot
2. Moses
3. Aaron
4. Isaac
5. Adam
6. Abraham
7. Caleb
8. Noe
9. Rebecca
10. Pharao

XVIII

CONDEMNED AGAIN TO WANDER

1. TURNED AWAY FROM THE LAND OF HOPE

The Israelites had arrived at the edge of the wonderful Land of Promise. They had suffered many hardships in traveling through the wilderness. Desert sands, the hot sun, dry wells, and lack of food, all helped to make their lives miserable. But the hope of one day entering the Promised Land gave them courage to bear these hardships. Now the land of hope was almost at their feet; yet they must turn their backs upon it and wander for forty years more in the wilderness. At the very moment of victory, they had refused to trust in God. The Lord had been good to them; He had been patient with their complaining; He had always listened to the prayers of Moses for them; He had led them through the desert. And now at

the end of their journey, they had lost faith in
Him. As a punishment, God said that all Israelites over twenty years of age, except Caleb and
Josue, would live and die in the wilderness and
would never see the Promised Land.

So with heavy hearts and saddened spirits,
they turned back into the desert. From place
to place they wandered. It was a dreary life.
For the older ones, there was no hope. As the
younger ones grew up, they heard sorrowful
stories of the trials of other days.

2. MOSES DISPLEASES GOD

It is strange that even the punishments of
God did not change the nature of Moses' followers. As the older people died and the younger
ones took their places, the same murmuring
and complaining was heard. At one time they
cried for water. God told Moses how to get
water from a certain stone near the camp. At
first Moses doubted. Later he gathered the
people together and spoke to them as if he were
going to bring water from the rock by his own

power. Twice he struck the rock with his rod, and water came pouring out.

But the conduct of Moses was not pleasing to God. Moses was giving honor and glory to himself and not to God. So the Lord said to him: "You did not do as I told you. You doubted My word and did not honor Me before the people. As a punishment for your actions, you will not enter the Promised Land." Adam and Eve disobeyed God and had to leave the Garden of Paradise. Moses disobeyed Him and lost the honor of leading the people into the land that God had promised to the children of Abraham.

3. THE DEATH OF AARON

This punishment was a terrible blow to Moses. Before long, other sorrows entered his life. The Angel of Death took his sister Mary from him. And shortly afterwards, God told him that the life of Aaron was fast coming to a close. God commanded Moses to go to the top of the mountain with Aaron and Aaron's oldest son, Eleazar.

Aaron was dressed in the beautiful robes of the high priest. He was weak, and found climbing the mountain a very difficult task. Moses and Eleazar helped him up the mountain. How

tired and weary the dying man was when they reached the top! Moses took the priest's robes from Aaron and placed them upon Eleazar, who was to be the new high priest. There on the mountain, far from friends and relatives, Aaron closed his eyes in death, and was buried by his son and his brother.

4. MURMURING AGAIN

When the forty years of punishment had almost passed, Moses started again with his people towards the Promised Land. One hot day, after a long walk over the desert sands, the Israelites set up their tents. They could find no water. The wells were dry, and no springs were in sight. Again they found fault with Moses, grumbling about all the hardships they had undergone. But their murmuring was really against God, because God was directing Moses.

Their constant grumbling angered the Lord. To punish them He sent snakes with poisonous bites into the camp. Men, women, and children fell dying upon the sand after being bitten. As usual the people turned to Moses for help. "We have sinned," they said, "because we have spoken against the Lord and you. Pray that He may take away these serpents from us." When trials and sufferings came upon them, they always knew where to look for help.

5. THE BRASS SERPENT

The meek and gentle Moses again prayed for the people, and the Lord said to him: "Make a serpent of brass and set it up in the camp.

When those who have been bitten look at it, they will be healed." Moses obeyed the command of God, and soon a brass serpent was placed upon a pole in the camp. How the people hurried to the pole to gaze upon the brass serpent! Fathers and mothers carried their dying children to look at the serpent, and strong sons helped fainting mothers and weeping sisters. All who looked with faith upon the serpent of brass were cured.

Suffering and death brought this sinful people to their senses. They confessed their fault, and said that they were sorry for their sins. Then God forgave them, and healed them through the brass serpent.

The serpent hanging on the pole represents Christ, Who hung upon the cross and saved the world from sin. In the world to-day, the serpent from hell—called *the devil*—goes about biting souls. His bite we call *sin*. In the days of old, nothing could save the people except looking at the brass serpent. To-day nothing can save them except faith and love for the Christ Who hung upon the cross.

COPY AND FILL THESE BLANKS

1. —— became high priest at the death of Aaron.
2. God punished the Israelites for their ——.
3. God told Moses how to get —— from a certain rock.
4. God sent poisonous —— to punish the Israelites.
5. The brass serpent represented ——.

XIX

THE DEATH OF THE LEADER

1. MOSES SPEAKS FOR THE LAST TIME

Finally the time came when Moses, too, must die. He was now one hundred and twenty years old. He had spent the first forty years of his life in Egypt at the palace of Pharao. For the next forty years, he had tended sheep on the hillsides of Madian. During the last forty years, he had been the leader of the Israelites. In spite of their complaining, the people really loved and respected Moses. His meek, gentle manner won the hearts of all.

The Israelites were now about to enter the Promised Land. But God had told Moses that he would never lead the people into the land of hope. So one day Moses gathered his followers together. He spoke to them about the greatness and glory of God. He reminded them of the many wonderful things that God had done for them.　He urged them to be faithful to God and to keep His commandments.

Then he said to them: "I am one hundred and twenty years old to-day.　I can no longer go in and come out as I used to.　God has forbidden

me to enter the Promised Land, but He has appointed Josue to lead you there."　He called Josue before all the people so that they would know that he was their new leader.　In the presence of the Israelites, he said to Josue: "Take courage and be brave, for you shall bring the people into the land that the Lord has promised to their fathers. You shall divide it by lot. And the Lord Who is your leader, He Himself will be with you. He will not forsake you. Fear not."

2. ON THE TOP OF THE MOUNTAIN

Then the grand old man bade the weeping people farewell. How sorry they were now that they had ever complained! How bitterly they regretted murmuring against him! Tear-filled eyes gazed upon the aged man as he slowly felt his way up the rocky footpath of Mount Nebo.

Their leader, their helper, their friend was leaving them forever.

God met Moses at the top of the mountain, and showed him the beauty and the richness of the Land of Promise. Then the Lord said to him: "This is the land that I promised to give to the children of Abraham, Isaac, and Jacob. You have seen it with your eyes but you shall not pass over it." Moses bowed to the will of God.

It was there on Mount Nebo that Moses, the great hero of Israel, died. God had His angels bury him, but no one has ever found the grave where they placed him. How dearly God loved this holy man, Moses, who was loyal, faithful, and true to the end!

THINGS TO FIND IN THE STORIES YOU HAVE READ BEFORE

1. Make a list of the stories which tell about Josue.
2. Find three events in the life of Moses which show his trust in God.
3. Find three conversations between God and Moses.
4. Find three events in the life of Moses which show his love for his people.

PART TWO

STORIES FROM THE NEW TESTAMENT

The great men about whom we have just been reading were chosen by God to direct His people and to make His will known to them while they were waiting for the coming of the One who was to make up for the sin of our first parents. Now we are going to read about this Redeemer, who, as we know, is Our Lord and Saviour, Jesus Christ.

XX

THE MESSAGE OF GOD'S ANGEL

1. THE ANNUNCIATION

Hidden away among the beautiful rolling hills, far removed from the noise and hurry of the larger cities, lay the peaceful village of Nazareth. Its inhabitants were poor, simple village folk. There was little to disturb the quiet life of this contented people. From day to day they went about their tasks, getting whatever joy they could out of life. Those who lived in the neighboring towns always looked down upon Nazareth — it was too small and humble for them.

In this secluded village lived two very happy people, Joseph and Mary. Joseph was a carpenter who worked daily in his little shop or helped his friends in their homes. He and Mary were poor; still they were of royal blood. They could trace their ancestors back to the great King David. Everybody in the village knew of the piety and goodness of Joseph and Mary. God's blessing would surely be with them.

One day, as Mary was kneeling in prayer, she heard a strange sound in the room. It seemed that some one had entered. Mary looked up,

and her eyes were dazzled by a brilliant light. "What can this be?" she thought. Soon she saw standing before her God's glorious angel, Gabriel. Was it any wonder, then, that the brightness dazzled her?

When the angel saw that she had recovered from her fright, he said, "Hail, full of grace, the Lord

is with thee; blessed art thou among women."
These words puzzled Mary. She did not know
what they meant. Why should she be blessed
among women? What kind of greeting was this?

The angel saw that Mary was overcome with
surprise, and that she did not understand his
words. Then he said to her, "Fear not, Mary,
for you have found favor with God. Behold
you shall give birth to a son, and you shall call
his name Jesus. He shall be great and shall be
called the Son of God."

"Can I believe my own ears or am I dreaming?"
thought Mary. "Is this a messenger from God
that stands before me?" Mary could not imagine
how this message could be true.

The angel Gabriel again assured her that she
would give birth to a son who would be called
the Son of God. He told her that the prayer of
her cousin Elizabeth was answered, and she also
would bring a little boy into the world. Mary
then bowed her head, and said, "Behold the
handmaid of the Lord. Be it done to me according to thy word."

2. MARY VISITS HER COUSIN ELIZABETH

Mary was glad to hear the good news about her cousin Elizabeth. She knew that both Elizabeth and her husband Zachary had prayed

many years for a little child. In her joy, Mary hastened to the home of her cousin. The journey was indeed a long one — up hill and down hill for many miles. But Mary's heart was too happy to notice the long weary journey.

As Mary entered the home of Elizabeth, her cousin clasped her in her arms. "Blessed art thou among women," she cried. "And whence is this to me that the mother of my God should come to me?"

Mary knew from these words that God had made known her secret to Elizabeth. She was filled with thoughts of God and in her joy she cried out, "My soul doth praise the Lord, and my spirit hath rejoiced in God, my Saviour, because He hath regarded the humility of His handmaid. For behold from henceforth all people shall call me blessed, because He that is mighty hath done great things to me, and holy is His name."

For three months Mary lived with her cousin, and both rejoiced in God's kindness to them.

COPY AND FILL THESE BLANKS

1. The people who lived in Nazareth were ———.
2. Joseph worked as a ———.
3. The angel first said to Mary ———.
4. Mary did not mind the long journey to Elizabeth because ———.
5. Elizabeth knew Mary's secret because ———.

XXI

THE BIRTH OF OUR KING

1. THE EDICT

"God save us from the Romans!"

"Why must we go to the city of our fathers?"

"What is it all about?"

"Oh, the cruel Roman emperor!"

"What a hard journey!"

It had been many a long day since the little village of Nazareth was so excited. Small groups gathered here and there along the main street of the town, talking loudly. Women came rushing to windows and doors to learn the cause of the noise and excitement.

The men of the town were just returning after having heard the reading of the Roman emperor's latest command. He wanted to find out just how many subjects he had, so he had ordered the people of the whole country to go to the city from which their fathers had come, and there

have their names placed upon the lists. These
lists would then be counted and the results
sent to him. He did not care if the people had
to walk ten miles or fifty miles. Neither did he
think of the many hardships that he was forcing
upon them.

It was no wonder that the quiet people of
Nazareth were excited. Of course, a few of them
looked upon their journey with pleasure, because
it gave them a chance to meet their friends and
relatives. For most of them, however, the order
meant a long, weary trip filled with hardships.

There was one man who did not linger with the crowds. He was Joseph, the carpenter. The news saddened him very much, but he thought to himself, "It is the law and must be obeyed." He feared to tell his wife Mary the bad news, but when she heard the order of the emperor she said mildly, "We shall obey."

2. THE JOURNEY TO BETHLEHEM

Plans were quickly made. The people gathered in small groups. In each group there were several donkeys to carry the little children, the women, and the food. Those going toward the west went in one group, those going toward the south in another. Among those traveling south were Joseph and Mary. They were going to Bethlehem, because they both belonged to the family of David, the great king who was born in Bethlehem.

It was a long, tiresome journey for Mary, even though she rode most of the way on one of the donkeys. Riding a donkey over a rough, stony road is not a pleasant thing. But she never complained. When Joseph thought that

she was tired, he would drop from the company
and rest with her along the roadside.

Some of the friends who left Nazareth with
Joseph and Mary withdrew from the group as
they passed through the towns of their families.

Others joined the company as it went from town
to town. When the tired travelers beheld the
gray walls of the city of Bethlehem rising from
the top of a distant hill, the men cheered with
joy. The end of a long and weary journey was
in view. They hastened their steps, in order to
arrive in the town before nightfall.

3. IN BETHLEHEM

The sun had already disappeared behind the hills and a cold evening breeze was blowing when the travelers reached the gates of Bethlehem. The gathering shades of twilight had grown deeper and deeper. A prayer of thanks rose from weary hearts. They had come to the end of the journey.

Bethlehem was all astir. There seemed to be crowds of people everywhere. Men, women, and children were talking and laughing, as they walked down the main street or gathered here and there in small groups. Friends and relatives who saw each other for the first time in years made the town ring with joy and mirth.

How could the little town hold all the people? Never before had such large numbers of men, women, and children passed through its gates. There were no great hotels nor large houses for the visitors. Many had made plans to spend the night in the homes of relatives or friends. Those who could not do this sought a place in the inn or little hotel. Very soon, however, the owner sent a message through the town, saying that he had no more room.

The pilgrims from distant Nazareth had arrived late. They hastened to the inn, but found no place to stay. The little group scattered in search of places to spend the night. Each family went its own way to find shelter.

The wintry winds that blew across the city were cold, sharp, and biting. Saint Joseph wrapped the Blessed Virgin's shawl closely around her to protect her from the chilly air. She remained near the gates of the city while Joseph went in search of a place for her. Up and down the streets he went, knocking at every door and begging for a place for Mary. As he passed from door to door, he always received the same answer, "We have no room."

Poor Saint Joseph was tired. His heart was heavy and sad. He did not think of himself but he thought of his dearly beloved Mary. He must find a home for her. He took the few coins that he had, and offered them at house after house. Many of the people of the town became angry and slammed the door in his face. Some of the kind people who saw Mary near the gate tried to find a home for her, but the task was hopeless.

Joseph was sorry for Mary when he saw that the darkness of night had settled over the town and he had found no place for her. He did not mind the harsh treatment he had received. He did not mind the insults which had been heaped upon him. But it grieved him to tell Mary that nobody wanted them because they were poor. The humble homes of Bethlehem little knew that they were turning the Lord of heaven and earth out into the cold world.

Almost in despair, Joseph approached a group of men standing near the gates of the city. He asked them if they knew of any place where Mary might spend the night. They had heard the same request from so many others that they paid no attention to it. But an old, old story tells of a little boy of twelve years who heard

Joseph speak to the men. He noticed the sad and disappointed look on Joseph's face, and saw about the head of Mary a strange light that made her appear very beautiful. He shyly

walked up to Joseph, and told him of a cave near the foot of a hill beyond the city gates.

These were the first kind words that Joseph had heard since his arrival in Bethlehem. It was now very dark, and Joseph did not know the way to the cave. The good boy was glad to go with him. Joseph placed Mary on the donkey. He led the tired animal by the halter, while the little boy walked ahead of them with a lantern in his hand. It seemed that Joseph's and Mary's only friends were the little boy and the stars twinkling in the sky above them. The story says that Jesus rewarded this boy for his kindness by giving him the gift of faith, and that later He called him to serve as a priest at the altar of God.

4. THE SAVIOUR IS BORN

Joseph and Mary entered the cave. How dark, damp, and cold it was! Joseph raised his lantern to look around. The cave was just a large room carved out of rock. From cracks here and there, could be heard the continual drip, drip, drip of the water as it fell upon the ground. In one corner was the manger — a rather large hole cut in the rock, where clean hay and straw were kept. Here Mary sat down to rest. In another part of the cave, an ox lay, quietly eating some hay. Joseph placed his donkey near the ox, and soon all was silent, without and within.

About midnight the cave suddenly brightened with a golden light. A sweet odor like perfume filled the air. The joyful music of angel voices was heard; for in that cave, Jesus, the Infant

Saviour, was born. The Lord God of heaven and earth came into the world as a tiny Babe in the cave at Bethlehem.

Joseph knelt in silent adoration before the Holy Child. Mary kissed her Child again and again with all the tenderness of a fond mother's love. The joy of heaven was in her heart as she gazed into the sweet face of the Infant Jesus.

He was her Child and she loved Him as her Son and her God.

Now, the Blessed Virgin had no lovely crib in which to place her little Babe and she had no pretty clothes to give Him. So she wrapped Him up in swaddling clothes and placed Him in the manger. Yes, a manger filled with straw in a cold, damp cave was the cradle of the Infant Jesus. A large cave dug in the side of a hill, a place without doors or windows, a shelter where the farmer kept his cows, was the first home of the Baby Jesus. How poor, how humble it was!

"The night is so cold," said Mary. "What shall I do to keep little Jesus warm?" She had already taken the shawl from her own shoulders and wrapped the Christ Child in it. But still He seemed cold. Just then the ox and the donkey walked over to the manger. They knelt before it and warmed the Holy Child with their breath. Sinful men had no place for Him in their homes in Bethlehem, but the ox and the donkey welcomed Him in their cave.

QUESTIONS

1. Why did the Roman emperor command the people to go to the city of their fathers?

2. Why did Joseph and Mary go to the town of Bethlehem?

3. Why was there no room for them in the town?

4. Tell about the cave in which Jesus was born.

5. Name some of the sufferings of the Infant Jesus.

XXII

ANGELS FROM HEAVEN

1. WAITING FOR THE SAVIOUR

For hundreds and hundreds of years, the world had been waiting for the coming of Christ, the Saviour. Many stories had been told about Him by the prophets and the leaders of the Jewish people. Again and again, in the temple, the people had listened to the priests as they spoke about the Redeemer who would come to save them.

Some thought that Christ would come as a great and glorious king. Others believed that He would come as a powerful general with a large army, to drive the Romans from the land of Israel. They all hoped that the great day would soon arrive when they would go forth to meet the Saviour of the people.

Little did they think that the Saviour would come as a tiny, poor, helpless Babe. Little did they dream that the Redeemer would be born in a cave, with no one to welcome Him with Mary and Joseph except the ox and the donkey. The Jews were looking for a Saviour surrounded with riches, pomp, and glory, — one they could greet with cheers and songs of praise.

But the ways of God are not like the ways of men. Our heavenly Father wanted to teach the world a lesson in humility that it would never forget. Therefore, He sent His divine Son into the world as an outcast, born of a poor but holy Virgin in a cold, dreary cave. No servants bowed before Him ready to obey His wishes. No great heralds with silver trumpets announced His coming in the marble palaces of the rich or in the great churches. No royal edict told the world of the birth of Christ, the King.

2. THE SHEPHERDS OF THE HILLS

On that first Christmas night, God looked down from His throne in heaven. He saw shepherds with their flocks on the hillsides outside

the city of Bethlehem.   These were good, simple,
honest men who spent their days and nights
with their sheep.   They loved their sheep, and
the sheep loved them.   They guarded them very
carefully from the attacks of roaming wild beasts.
Sometimes hungry wolves would lie still in the
forests all day, and at night sneak out to the
sheepfold, and carry a little lamb away to the
woods.   Therefore, during the night one shepherd always kept watch while the others slept.

It was a peaceful scene that God looked upon.
The sleeping sheep were huddled together and
in the moonlight appeared like a rolling field
of gray.   Now and then, flames leaped from
the camp fires and showed the faces of tired
shepherds who dozed upon the ground wrapped
in blankets.   One silent form slowly wandered
about the sheepfold.   It was the shepherd on
watch.

God thought to Himself that He would make
known the birth of the Saviour to these poor
honest men first.   He sent His angels with the
glad news.   The shepherds were suddenly roused

by a dazzling, bright light. Trembling in fear, they gazed at one another. The frightened men wondered what was going to happen. The sheep thought that morning had come and greeted it with their gentle bleating.

3. THE MESSAGE FROM HEAVEN

The shepherds gathered together to help and protect one another. The sky above them seemed to have opened, letting fall a shower of golden brightness upon the earth. Soon a beautiful angel, shining in glory, was seen standing in the bright light. The angel noticed how frightened the poor shepherds were, so he spoke in a kind, low voice. "Fear not," he said, "for behold, I bring you good tidings of great joy that shall be to all the people. For this day is born to you a Saviour, who is Christ the Lord, in the city of David. And this shall be a sign to you: you shall find the Infant wrapped in swaddling clothes and laid in a manger."

The shepherds thought that they were dreaming. The Lord and Saviour born in Bethlehem? Yes, they had all heard it. While they were still wondering, a great number of angels appeared in the sky, praising God and singing, "Glory to God in the highest; and on earth, peace to men of good will." Such sweet music had never before been heard on earth. It was God's own choir. Then fainter and fainter the voices sounded, as the angels faded in the deep blue sky.

When the blackness of night returned, and the music of the angels had died away in the distance, the shepherds stood in silence. Then they said, "Let us go over to Bethlehem, and let us see this word that is come to pass, which the Lord has shown us." In their eagerness they did not wait for morning, but immediately

hastened over the hill to the cave where they found Mary and Joseph watching over the Infant Jesus lying in the manger.

They told Joseph and Mary about the message of the angel and the beautiful choir from heaven that God had sent to announce the birth of Jesus. They knelt in prayer before the tiny

Infant in the manger, adoring Him as their God and Saviour.

The shepherds lost no time in spreading the startling news throughout the town of Bethlehem. The birth of Christ the Lord was made known to all they met. The people wondered at the stories about the angels told by the shepherds from the hills.

SENTENCES TO COPY

When you copy these sentences, choose the right word only in the places where two words are given.

1. The Jews thought that the Saviour would be born in a (*palace, cave*).

2. The shepherds were watching their (*sheep, wolves*).

3. The (*angels, shepherds*) sang, "Glory to God in the highest."

4. God first told the news of Our Lord's birth to (*the king, poor shepherds*).

5. The shepherds told their great news to (*every one, no one*).

XXIII

THE WISE MEN FROM THE EAST

1. NEWS FROM THE EAST

Some time after the shepherds made their midnight visit to the Infant Jesus, a very interesting sight appeared at the gates of Jerusalem. Three large camels stood there with rich robes of crimson, blue, and gold thrown across their backs. Upon each of the camels sat a stately prince clad in the beautiful flowing garments of the East. Indeed they made a very pretty picture with their dark skin and their bright-colored clothes. They were the Wise Men from the East.

They asked the keeper of the gate: "Where is He that is born King of the Jews? We have seen His star in the East and are come to adore Him."

"King of the Jews!" said the keeper. "He is called Herod, but many a year has passed since he was born."

187

The Wise Men then explained that they were looking for a new-born babe who was to be the King of the Jews.

The gate-keeper knew all the gossip of the town, but he had not heard of the birth of any king. He called to some of his friends who were standing near and asked them about the new babe that had been born. They stroked their long beards and shook their heads. They had heard nothing of this new king. The Wise Men, or *Magi*, as they were sometimes called, were disappointed. They had followed a new bright star that had appeared in the eastern sky. The star had led them as far as Jerusalem. They had expected everybody here to know about the new-born king.

2. BEFORE KING HEROD

As the visitors passed through the narrow streets of the city, men, women, and children rushed from their homes to see them. Most of the people had never seen such princely figures. They gazed in reverent awe as the stately parade slowly passed down the streets. Now and then, the Wise Men halted their camels and asked the people if they knew where the new-born king could be found. But no one was able to help them.

King Herod soon found out that three Wise Men from the East were asking for the new-born King of the Jews. The thought of another king for the Jews angered Herod. He made up his mind that no other king should take his throne

from him.   He decided to find out more about
this king.

He called a meeting of the chief priests in the
royal palace.   He knew that they would be able
to tell him something.   He had often heard the
Jews speak about a king that God was to send
to save them.   But he had paid little attention
to the stories.   Now he called together the
learned men of the Jews, and asked them where
this king should be born.   They told him that
the holy writings said that the new King of the
Jews would be born in Bethlehem.

King Herod then secretly sent his soldiers
to the Wise Men, asking them to meet him in the
royal palace.   The visitors were delighted because
they thought that the king would be able to
help them.   They bowed before Herod as he
sat upon his throne.   Herod was much interested
in their story.   He inquired carefully about the
star they had seen, and asked when it had first
appeared.   Then he told them that the Child
they were seeking would be found in Bethlehem.
"Go and carefully inquire after the Child," he

said, "and when you have found him, bring me word again that I also may come and adore him."

The Wise Men were pleased with the king. They thought that he was a very kind ruler who wished to worship the new-born king. Little did they think that Herod was planning to destroy the Child.

3. THE NEW BORN KING IS FOUND

An escort of soldiers quietly led the Wise Men from the palace of Herod to the gates of the city, and pointed out to them the road to Bethlehem. To their great joy, the star again appeared and went before them till it stood over the spot where the Child was. They entered the house, and there they found the Child with Mary, His mother. When they saw Him they fell down and adored Him. Then they opened their treasures and offered Him gifts — gold, incense, and myrrh.

Mary was indeed surprised when these richly dressed men entered her home. Clothes such as they wore were not known in her part of the country. With bowed heads they knelt before the crib and worshiped the Infant lying in a sweet sleep. They had traveled over a dusty road for several weeks to have the honor of kneeling by the crib of Christ, the new-born King.

They opened their jeweled boxes, and offered the Infant their gifts. With their gold, they

recognized Jesus as their King; with their incense they recognized Him as their God; with their myrrh they recognized Him as the Man who was later to suffer and to die. With happy hearts, they spread their gifts before the crib of Jesus. Their prayers had been answered; they had seen Christ, the Saviour.

That night while they were sleeping, an angel appeared to them and told them not to return to Herod because he was seeking to kill the Child. At dawn the next morning they set out for home. However they did not take the road through Jerusalem. Travelers pointed out to them a road that led them back to their home country by another way.

ARE THESE TRUE OR FALSE?

1. The Wise Men had followed a star to Jerusalem.
2. The Wise Men came from the East.
3. The gate-keeper told the Wise Men where to find the new-born king.
4. Herod wished to adore the new-born king.
5. The Wise Men brought Jesus gifts of gold, incense, and myrrh.
6. An angel told the Wise Men to return to Herod.

XXIV

THE FLIGHT INTO EGYPT

1. THE ANGEL'S WARNING

Soon after the Wise Men had started on their homeward journey, an angel appeared to Joseph and said to him, "Arise, and take the Child and His mother, and fly into Egypt. And be there until I shall tell you. For it will come to pass that Herod will seek the Child to destroy Him."

Joseph hurriedly wakened Mary. She gathered up the few clothes they had, while Joseph brought the donkey to the door. Mary sat upon the donkey, holding the sleeping Jesus in her arms. Joseph walked beside them, leading the animal by the halter.

The sweet little Jesus, only a few weeks old, had to be taken to a distant land to save His life. Imagine the Holy Family, starting out in the stillness of night, with only the stars looking on in a friendly way. Time and again,

Joseph had to hurry the donkey along, because he feared that Herod's soldiers might follow them.

It was a long, weary journey for Mary. But for the safety of her Child, she gladly suffered. Hunger and thirst did not bother her as long as Jesus was safe. For years they were to live among strangers in a strange land, until at last the angel called them back to their own country.

2. HEROD'S CRUEL ORDER

Herod grew impatient waiting for the return of the Wise Men. He could not imagine why they delayed so long. Finally he could wait no longer, so he sent some of his soldiers to Bethlehem to inquire about the Wise Men. When they brought him news that the Wise Men had long ago left Bethlehem, he became very angry. When he realized that he had been tricked, his rage increased.

In his anger, he commanded his soldiers to kill every baby boy in Bethlehem who was two years old or younger. The brutal soldiers mounted their horses and galloped to Bethlehem. With sword in hand, they went through the town. Bitter sorrow filled the homes of Bethlehem, where the tiny innocent children lay dead. But in Jerusalem, a savage king rejoiced, because he thought that he had made his throne secure. Herod felt sure that the new-born king was among those who had been killed by his soldiers. He did not know that God's angels were guarding the life of the Infant Jesus, and that at that very time they were leading Him safely to the land of Egypt.

3. THE RETURN TO NAZARETH

The Holy Family remained in Egypt for some time. At last an angel came to Joseph in a dream and said to him, "Arise and take the Child and His mother and return to the land of Israel, for those who wished to kill the Child are dead."

Mary and Joseph started at once on the homeward journey. How happy they were to know that the little Jesus was now safe! As they drew near their native land, they heard that although Herod was dead, his son, who was as cruel as his father, ruled in his place. They hurried on, eager to reach Nazareth, where they would be at a distance from the wicked king.

They were very glad to be back in their humble little home once more and to be among their friends. The home of the Holy Family at Nazareth is an example of what our homes should be. We should imitate the boy Jesus by our obedience, gentleness, and kindness, and we should love and help our parents as He loved and helped Mary and Joseph.

QUESTIONS

1. Why did the angel tell Joseph to go to Egypt?
2. Give some reasons why the journey to Egypt was difficult.
3. Why was Herod angry when he heard that the Wise Men had left?
4. Why did he command his soldiers to kill all the baby boys?
5. Was his plan successful?

XXV

LOST IN THE TEMPLE

1. THE JOURNEY TO JERUSALEM

Jerusalem was the holy city of the Jews. Here stood the beautiful marble temple where the priests daily offered sacrifice to God. Here the people came year after year to celebrate the great feasts of the Jewish religion. It was the custom of Joseph and Mary to make a yearly journey to Jerusalem to celebrate the feast of the Passover. Can you tell the story of the first feast of the Passover?

When Jesus was twelve years old, His parents brought Him with them to celebrate this feast. The boy Jesus enjoyed the trip. Many friends and relatives from Nazareth were with them. The women rode part of the way on donkeys that were led by men or boys. Perhaps Jesus led the donkey when His Blessed Mother was riding. We can well imagine how carefully He picked the smooth parts of the road and how kindly He urged the donkey onward. In the evenings, the whole company pitched their tents near some well or stream. Joyful boys ran here and there gathering wood for the fires or carrying water.

After a few days of travel, they reached Jerusalem. How happy Jesus was as He entered the gates of the holy city! Mary and Joseph had often told Him about its wonders, and now He was in the midst of them.

2. THE TEMPLE

The Temple was one of the most beautiful buildings that the world has ever seen. Four marble courts of wonderful splendor rose one above the other. Those who did not believe in the God of Israel were permitted to enter the first court, but it meant death to them if they went beyond it. The women worshiped in the second court, unless they were bringing a sacrifice to the altars. Men and women never

worshiped together in the Jewish temples, so
the men had the next court for themselves. The
highest court, which was the Court of the Priests,
was the richest and most beautiful part of the
Temple. Glistening gold and sparkling jewels

dazzled the eyes. Here was the altar of sacrifice,
the altar of incense, and the Holy of Holies.

The temple was the dearest place on earth to
every Jewish heart. To pray within its walls
brought peace and happiness to the troubled soul.
How dear to our hearts should be our churches,
because they contain the living God Himself,

and not merely His altars or His laws as did the Jewish temple!

Jesus was delighted to be in God's house, because it was His house also. The great feast lasted a week, and each day Jesus went to the temple with Saint Joseph. He saw the pious little altar boys who helped the priests around the temple. He watched the white-robed priests as they slowly passed in and out of the holy place. He was happy, very happy indeed.

3. JESUS REMAINS IN JERUSALEM

After the celebration was over, the pilgrims began to leave the city. All those going toward Nazareth decided to journey together. It was never safe to travel along the lonely roads in small parties. Robbers of the meanest kind often lay in wait for the weary travelers to take from them their food, money, and everything else of value. In the land where Jesus lived, things have not changed very much since those days, for even in our own times it is not safe to travel there in small groups without armed guides.

When the hour of departure arrived, all the people going in the direction of Nazareth had not assembled. Some of the party, therefore, started without waiting for the rest. Joseph was among these. Later the second group followed them. The Blessed Virgin and some of her friends were in this group. Mary did not see the first group depart, so she thought that Jesus was with Saint Joseph. And Joseph naturally thought that Jesus was with His mother.

The happy people traveled on for the whole day, talking about the beautiful temple, the solemn services of the priests, and about the many relatives and friends they had met during the week. It was a lovely day for walking. The air was sweet with the breath of the first blossoms of spring. When the darkness of night made traveling impossible, the first group selected a pretty spot covered with grass, where they pitched their tents. Joseph had fixed his tent, filled the jars with water, and started a fire by the time the second group arrived.

Mary looked anxiously around for Jesus and

did not see Him. "Where is Jesus?" she asked.

Joseph stared at her in amazement. "Jesus?" he said. "I thought that He was with you."

"And I thought that He was with you," said Mary as her eyes filled with tears. "My boy, my boy is lost!" she cried.

Mary and Joseph hurried through the camp to find Jesus, but He was nowhere to be found. The heart of Mary was filled with terror. She blamed herself for not being more watchful.

Back to Jerusalem, Mary and Joseph hastened. Their feet and the tired donkey could not carry them fast enough. They imagined that all sorts of things had happened to Jesus. They thought that perhaps He had been killed or stolen. Perhaps He had walked with another party in the opposite direction.

Through the streets of Jerusalem they hurried, asking everyone they met, "Have you seen our boy Jesus?" No one had seen Him. They called at the home of their relatives, but Jesus had not been there. They went to the houses of their friends, but Jesus was not to be found.

4. FOUND AT LAST

Oh, how they prayed that God would save His Son! After three days' searching, Joseph and Mary entered the temple. There to their joy and amazement, they saw the child Jesus talking to the Jewish doctors, asking them questions, and by His answers putting to shame the wisdom of old men.

The joy of the Blessed Virgin was so great that she burst into tears, and threw her arms around her boy saying: "Why have you done so to us? Behold your father and I have sought you sorrowing."

Jesus did not like to see His mother in sorrow so He kissed away her tears. Then He said

some strange words to her: "How is it that you sought me? Did you not know that I must be about my Father's business?"

The Blessed Virgin and Saint Joseph did not understand what Jesus meant. They did not know that He was speaking about the great work for which He came into the world, — the work of saving men's souls. The Jewish doctors told Joseph that Jesus was a wonderful boy. They were astonished at the things that He knew.

Joseph embraced the child Jesus, and the Holy Family began their return trip to Nazareth. This quiet little village was to be Jesus' home for the next eighteen years. There He lived with Joseph and Mary, loving them and obeying them.

Jesus, the Son of God, was a beautiful example of obedience to all boys and girls. He loved His mother so dearly that He did all in His power to make her happy. He helped her about their little home, and He helped Saint Joseph in the carpenter shop. The little boy Jesus is our model. Let us learn from Him to honor, obey, and love our parents.

ANSWER THESE QUESTIONS

1. How were the people divided in the temple?
2. Explain how Jesus became lost.
3. What was Jesus doing when His parents found Him?
4. Why could Jesus answer the questions of the learned doctors so well?
5. In what special way is the boy Jesus our model?

XXVI

A WEDDING GIFT FROM JESUS

1. OUR LORD BEGINS HIS PUBLIC WORK

In the last story we read that after Jesus was found in the temple, He went with His parents to their humble home in Nazareth. There in the quiet village He lived until He was thirty years old.

The time had now come when Jesus must begin the work for which He had come into the world. He bade farewell to the mother He loved so well. He cast a fond look about the neat little home that He was leaving forever, the home where He had spent so many years in peace and happiness with Joseph and Mary.

Our Lord was soon baptized in the Jordan River by His cousin, John the Baptist. Later He went into the desert alone to fast and pray for forty days. There He spoke with His heavenly

Father. In this way, He prepared Himself for His work.

Leaving the desert, He began to preach to the people. From time to time, He selected disciples or companions to help Him. The warmth of His love for the people soon showed itself in His teaching, and before long they learned to love Him.

2. AT THE MARRIAGE FEAST

It was in these early days of His public work that He was invited to a marriage feast in Cana. The bride or her husband was probably related to the family of Joseph or Mary. They were poor, simple people in the things of the world but good and holy in the sight of God.

Jesus brought His disciples with Him to the marriage feast. His mother, Mary, had arrived long before, and was helping the bride. Oh! how happy she was to embrace Her divine Son again! The bride and groom were pleased that Jesus and His friends had honored their poor home by attending the feast. Jesus blessed them, and wished them many years of happiness.

The neighbors, bringing little gifts with them, came in small groups to greet the newly married couple. All were invited to remain for the feast. Peals of laughter and songs of joy echoed and re-echoed through the house as the guests enjoyed the wedding dinner.

Soon the Blessed Virgin whispered something to Her Son. She did it so quietly that only a few in the room noticed her. What was she saying? She had discovered that the wine was almost gone. The expenses of the feast had been so great that the poor people had not bought enough wine to serve the guests. The Blessed Virgin saw that the bridal couple looked worried. They were afraid that soon their friends would find out that they had not enough wine for the feast. Mary pitied them, so she said to Jesus, "Son, they have no wine."

3. THE FIRST PUBLIC MIRACLE OF JESUS

The mother of Jesus knew the power of her divine Son. She also knew that He would be pleased to help these poor people. Jesus answered her gently, saying that the time for Him to perform His first public miracle had not yet come. Perhaps He meant that all the people at the banquet must know that the wine had given out before He performed His first miracle.

But Mary was sure that Jesus would do something for the bridal party. She went to those who were serving the dinner and said to them, "Do whatever He shall say to you."

Jesus soon gathered His flowing white robes about Him and rose from the table. So quietly did He move that no one noticed Him, except those who were sitting near Him. He looked around the room made bright by the flickering light of yellow candles. Near the door He saw six earthenware jars, each large enough to hold about one hundred quarts. These were left near the entrance of the house to supply the water with which visitors washed their hands and feet before they sat down to eat. Do you remember how Abraham brought water to wash the feet of his three guests?

Our Lord told the men to fill the jars with

water. When they had done so He blessed the
jars. At His blessing, the water was suddenly
changed into wine of the most delicious flavor.

Jesus then said to one of those serving the guests,
"Bring a cup of this wine to the man in charge
of the feast."

When this man tasted the new wine, he called
out loudly to the bridegroom: "Why have you
saved the best wine till the end of the feast?
Generally people serve the best wine first and
the poorer wines later on, but you have saved
the best for the end." The speaker did not know

that the wine he was praising had been made by God Himself. It was a wedding present from the Lord. Was it any wonder that it had such a fine flavor?

The truth was now made known that Jesus of Nazareth had changed the water into wine. Eyes opened wide with surprise. The excited people gathered in little groups, and began to whisper, "Who is this Jesus? Is he not the son of Mary from Nazareth? How could he change the water into wine?" They did not know that Jesus was the Son of God, but they did know that He had a power that came from God only.

This was Jesus' first public miracle, a miracle performed at the request of His Blessed Mother. It shows us the eagerness of the Blessed Virgin to appeal to her divine Son for those in need. The tender heart of Mary was filled with sympathy for the bridal couple when she saw that there was no more wine for the guests. That same heart is anxious to help us in all our trials and sorrows. Mary is always glad to kneel before the throne of Jesus and plead for us. In her, we have a heavenly mother who loves us with all the sweetness and tenderness of our own mothers. Let us then kneel before the shrine of Mary and offer her our fervent prayers, asking her to speak to Jesus for us.

COPY AND FILL IN THE BLANKS

1. Jesus was baptized by ———.
2. Jesus prepared for His public work by ———.
3. The Blessed Virgin spoke to Jesus about the wine because ———.
4. This miracle shows us ———.

XXVII

THE GREAT HEALER OF CAPHARNAUM

1. THE CITY JESUS LOVED

Jesus loved Capharnaum, the beautiful city by the sea. He loved it not for its palaces and riches, but because of the warm-hearted people who made their homes there. The simple life of these good people made them very dear to Him. Many of them spent their days on farms, tilling the soil, sowing the seed, and reaping the harvest. Others gave their time to fishing in the deep waters of the sea. During their spare hours, they sat in groups along the shore, and mended their nets or sold their fish.

Jesus enjoyed walking through the farm country. He often paused to talk with the farmers, as they scattered their seed or gathered in the fruits of the harvest. In the evenings, when the rays of the dying sun gilded the dancing waves, He often sat by the seashore to see the fishermen bring the day's catch to shore. Jesus chose some of these good, earnest men to be His closest friends and disciples.

But Our Lord was scarcely ever alone. As soon as His pleasant face and graceful form appeared in the city, the people flocked around Him. Many came to hear Him speak. Others came to find fault with Him or with His teaching. And near Him could always be found those who were looking for a cure from some affliction.

The blind, the deaf, the dumb, the crippled, and the fevered were sure to find their way to Jesus. Those who could not walk were carried or helped by friends. The tender heart of the Lord melted with pity for them. The touch of His hand healed them, and a blessing from His lips sent them away smiling.

2. CROWDS GATHER TO SEE THE MASTER

On a lovely day in September, Jesus stopped at one of the larger homes of the city. The low, whitewashed house with its flat roof stood in the

middle of a large yard. The ground was covered
with crisp, brown leaves that the autumn winds
had blown from the oak and olive trees growing
near by. Withering vines crept up the sides of

the house and almost hid from view the stair-
way that led to the roof.

The news that Jesus was visiting in the neighborhood brought all the people from the sur-
rounding cottages to see Him. Soon the house
was filled. Those who arrived late gathered
in the yard. "Make room! Make room!"

shouted four men carrying a crippled friend upon a mat. The crowd looked at them with sympathy, but no man made room. They all wanted to get near the Lord. The four men again pleaded for space that they might bring their friend to the feet of the Master. But no one moved. Then in their eagerness, they began to force their way, but found the crowd too great.

"What shall we do? We cannot get through the crowd," said a man with a long gray beard, who appeared to be the leader of the little group of friends.

"Let us return home. It is hopeless to try to do anything," answered a red-faced youth with a disappointed look. When the poor cripple on the mat heard his friends talking about going home, he begged them in the name of mercy to help him in his sorrow.

Then a third member of the party spoke up: "If we cannot bring our friend in through the door, why not let him in through the roof? The tiles are easily removed, and with strong rope we can let the mat down from the roof to the floor of the house.

"Thank God!" murmured the poor, sick man who was trembling with a disease called *palsy*.

3. THE SICK MAN IS CURED

The four men were happy at the idea of placing their suffering friend at the feet of Jesus. Rope was found in a corner of the yard. With a little effort, they carried up the narrow stairs the mat on which their friend lay. The precious burden was carefully set down in a corner. The men then quickly removed the tiles. The people in the house were amazed when they looked up and saw what their neighbors were doing. As soon as a hole large enough was made, the men tied ropes to the corners of the mat and slowly lowered their friend to the floor of the room where Jesus was speaking.

Imagine the surprise of the people when they beheld the crippled man coming down from the roof on a mat! "Have pity on me! Have pity on me!" murmured the poor man as he came near Jesus. He did not need to tell Jesus what he wanted. One look at that trembling, suffering body and those pitiful eyes was enough.

Our Lord admired the strong faith of the sick man and his friends, so He said in a soft, kind voice, "Son, thy sins are forgiven thee." The happiness that Our Lord's message brought showed in the face of the man lying on the mat. He knew that he had done many things that offended God, and now those sins were all forgiven. How often we have the same happy feeling after confession when the priest washes the stains from our souls!

4. JESUS SILENCES HIS ENEMIES

Some of the enemies of Jesus who were standing near, lifted their eyebrows, and nodded to one another saying, "Why does this man speak thus? Who can forgive sin, but God only?"

Jesus was truly God, and He could read the thoughts that were in the minds of His enemies. He said to them, "Why do you think evil in your hearts? Which is easier to say, 'Thy sins are forgiven thee,' or to say, 'Arise, take up thy bed and walk'?'' Then He told them that He would show them that the Son of Man had the power on earth to forgive sin. He turned to the sick man and said, "Arise, take up thy bed, and go into thy house."

The trembling limbs immediately became still. New life seemed to shoot through the body. In his joy, the man sprang to his feet. He rolled up his mat, placed it upon his shoulders, and left the house rejoicing with his friends.

The crowds gazed in wonder. The enemies of Christ quickly disappeared behind the cheering people, who praised God saying, "How wonderful is Jesus of Nazareth!"

COPY AND COMPLETE THESE SENTENCES

1. Jesus loved Capharnaum because ——.
2. People flocked around Jesus because ——.
3. It was easy for the men to let their friend down through the roof because ——.
4. The sick man did not need to tell Jesus what he wanted because ——.
5. This story shows the power of ——.

XXVIII

JESUS AND THE LITTLE CHILDREN

1. THE WEARY TRAVELERS

The soft glow of early evening had settled over the hills of Judea when Jesus and His Apostles were seen on the highway. Their sandals were covered with dust, and their slow, weary steps gave signs that the travelers had come from afar.

They had walked from the shores of Lake Galilee. Jesus loved this beautiful lake. But now He had left His favorite place to preach to the people of Judea.

Jesus and His companions sat down to rest near an old stone well just outside the walls of the city. A young woman of the town came to the well to fill her jars with water. When she saw Jesus and His friends, she hastened to tell the people of the town that the Master had come. Everybody was eager to see the Man Who had made the lame walk and the blind see.

The Apostles were very tired, and they knew that Jesus was more tired than they, for He had spent the night in prayer. They spoke to the people, and tried to send them back to their homes. But the people paid no attention to them. They had come to see Jesus and to hear Him, and nothing could turn them away.

Mothers carrying sick children forced their way through the crowd, so that Jesus might bless their little ones. The blind, holding tightly to their leaders, pushed others aside in their efforts to have the good Master place His hand upon their eyes.

Jesus was never too tired to help the needy. He was never too weary to listen to the prayers of those who suffered. Finally, the talking of the crowd died away, and Jesus began to speak. How eagerly the people listened to every word that fell from His holy lips!

2. SUFFER THE CHILDREN TO COME UNTO ME

Eager little boys and girls stood in the crowd but could see nothing. They were almost buried among the grown folks. They could hear the kind voice of the Master, but they wanted to see His face and hold His hand. Some of the braver ones worked their way through the crowd to the very feet of Jesus. They shyly placed their arms around Him as He tenderly embraced them.

Others, sitting on the shoulders of their fathers or peeking through the crowd, saw their playmates near Jesus. They also wanted to go to Him. More began to make their way toward Jesus. This angered the Apostles and many of the older people. They roughly pushed the children back, and told them to go home. The Apostles told the mothers to take their children away, because they were bothering the Master.

Our Lord heard the sharp voices of the men, and soon the sobbing of children reached His ears. He asked what was the matter. When

He was told that the men were driving the children away, He called the children to Him. He told the men to stand back and make way for them. The people never forgot His words. "Suffer the little children to come unto Me and forbid them not, for of such is the kingdom of God," He said.

3. JESUS AND HIS LITTLE FRIENDS

Smiles covered the faces of the little ones as they gathered about the Lord. Children in red, blue, green, and gold tunics clamored to kiss the hand of Jesus. Now and then He took a crippled child from the arms of its mother, kissed it, and gave it back to her cured. He twisted His slender fingers in and out among the curls of some of the little girls.

He embraced them lovingly and kissed them one and all. Some sat at His feet and looked into His kind, sweet face. Others placed their arms about Him. A few just stood before Him and gazed in silent awe. They loved the gentle Jesus, and Jesus loved them.

The Apostles and many of the others thought that Jesus was wasting His time on these little children. The older people wanted Jesus to talk to them. Now, Jesus was God, and He knew what they were thinking. So He took a little child from the crowd, and placed it upon a stone near by. Then He preached a sermon to the people, telling them that unless they became as little children, they could not enter the kingdom of heaven. Our Lord looks upon little children as pure, good and holy. As they grow older He wants them to keep like that.

4. JESUS BLESSES US FROM THE ALTAR

Our dear Lord loves all children. He is always ready to hear their prayers and to give them His blessing. How would you like to have been with the little children whom Jesus kissed and blessed? You can have the same honor if you wish. God rests on the altar of your Church just as truly as He rested near the town of Judea. By making a little visit to Him in the Sacrament of His Love, you can talk to Him as freely as did the children of Judea, and He will give you the same blessing he gave to them.

READ THE PART OF THE STORY THAT TELLS

1. How the people knew that Jesus was there.
2. Why the Apostles wished to send the people away.
3. How Jesus showed that He loved little children.
4. How you can talk to Our Lord as the children in this story did.

PART THREE
HEROES IN GOD'S CHURCH

There are many other beautiful stories about the life of Our Lord.   But now we are going to read stories from the lives of God's friends, the Saints.   They will be glad to be our friends, too, if we ask them, and whatever our age or our state of life, we shall find among the Saints someone whom we can love and imitate.

XXIX

THE FEARLESS SAINT

1. MARTYRS IN THE EARLY CHURCH

In the early days of the Church, the heartless rulers of Rome considered it a crime to believe in Our Lord. Time and again, they gave orders to their soldiers to capture and put to death all those who believed in the God Who made heaven and earth. Thousands and thousands of Christians were cruelly tortured and killed because they loved Jesus and tried to serve Him. Those who gave up their lives for the sake of our dear Lord are called *martyrs*.

In this world the martyrs suffered imprisonment, torture, and death because they loved God. Our Heavenly Father has rewarded them, and now they are happy with Him in His kingdom.

Sometimes, in those terrible days, officers in the army, and men and women of high rank

were put to death because they were Christians.
The Roman soldiers had no need to go out and
search for the brave St. George. His wisdom
and bravery had won him promotion after promotion in the army. The emperor admired his
faithful captain and had shown him many signs
of friendship. However, as soon as the emperor
sent out his commands against the Christians,
the noble heart of George felt that it could no
longer serve the enemy of his God.

2. ST. GEORGE DIES FOR THE FAITH

George went to the emperor and said to him:
"I am a Christian. No longer can I be a soldier
of him who hates the God of the Christians."
Then taking the shield from his breast and the
sword from his belt, he continued, "At your
feet I place the gifts you gave me, because I
will not use them against God's people."

The emperor laughed at the soldier he loved.
He thought that this foolish notion would
soon leave the mind of the bravest man in his
guard. "Go, my friend," he said, "and offer

incense to our Roman gods. Forget your foolish notions."

But St. George refused to be sent away so easily. He informed the emperor that he had been serving the God of the Christians in secret

for a long time. This news made the emperor angry, and he commanded the guards to cast George into prison. Here he was brutally treated. In his suffering Our Lord comforted him and said to him, "Fear not, for I am with you."

The Emperor promised St. George his freedom

if he would give up his faith.   But the soldiers reported to the emperor that nothing could shake the faith of his former favorite.   The sentence of death was then pronounced.   Soon St. George was numbered with the saints in heaven.

3.   THE FEROCIOUS DRAGON

A very interesting story is told of St. George's battle with a dragon.   This ugly monster had eyes that flashed fire, and rows of large, pointed teeth.   Often it would dash through the woods, tearing up by the roots trees that stood in its way.   For years it had lived on the other animals of the forest, and its hunger was so great that most of the other wild animals had now disappeared.   It began to attack the herds of cattle and the flocks of sheep.   Young calves and sheep were its food for many a day.   But even this did not satisfy the terrible dragon.   It began to eat men, women, and children.

The poor people were angry when the dragon stole the calves and sheep from their flocks. But imagine how frantic they became when this beast of the forest began to eat the people! For a long time they did not know what to do. Finally they made an agreement to send daily to the dragon two sheep.

Things went well as long as the sheep were sent to the den of this monster. But after some time, there were no more sheep to send, and the calves had long ago disappeared. What could the frightened people do?

They decided on a plan which seems terrible to us. They agreed to send to the dragon each day two children, to be drawn by lot. What a dreadful sentence of death to give to the innocent children! Mothers wept bitterly, and the hearts of fathers were broken with grief, as they kissed their little ones good-bye before they were placed outside the city gates to be the food of the dragon.

4. A BRAVE GIRL

Finally, the lot fell upon the daughter of the ruler of the city. The news was a shock to him. He had seen the daughters of other men go forth to death, but had thought little of it.

Now that his own beloved daughter was doomed, he rebelled.

But the people of the town stormed about his home, and demanded that there be no exception. The choice by lot was final, whether it fell upon the daughter of the ruler or the daughter of the pauper. The ruler pleaded for his child, but the angry people paid no attention to him. The girl, however, had a nobler and braver nature than her father. She said to him very calmly, "I shall gladly give myself for the people."

The people of the town really loved this heroic girl. They were half inclined to choose another in her place. But the girl had made up her mind that she was not to be an exception to the rule.

Her day of fate finally came. She appeared at the gates of the city dressed in a flowing white dress, with her brown hair falling in curls to her waist. Many of the townsfolk had come to bid her farewell. Her grief-stricken father kissed her over and over again. The feeble old keeper of the gates regretfully opened them. The girl passed through and gave a fond last look at her weeping friends. The gates were closed again. The sad-hearted people thought that they had seen the girl for the last time.

When the gates were closed, the doomed girl gave way to her feelings and wept bitterly. Until now, for her father's sake, she had kept her courage in a wonderful manner. Now, alone on her way to death, she did not need to care.

5. SAVED FROM DEATH BY ST. GEORGE

Slowly the white-clad figure passed along the footpath that led to the swampy part of the forest to which the dragon carried his prey. Suddenly she was startled by the sound of a horse's hoofs. She turned around and saw a soldier on a large white horse, galloping toward the gates of the city. Knowing that he would have to cross her path, she dried her eyes and tried to smile.

The rider stopped his horse on the road in front of the girl. The soldier wondered where this pretty child was going. He asked her a

question or two, and the poor girl could hide
her tears no longer. She told him the story of
the dragon and the casting of lots. Imagine his
amazement when she told him that she was on
her way to death!

The soldier could not understand how the
men in the town would permit such an outrage.
He said to the girl, "Wait here and I shall slay
this monster." The brave girl begged him to
hurry to the city lest he too should die. But
fear was never known to enter the heart of St.
George, for such was the name of the soldier.

St. George made the sign of the cross, and called upon God to come to his help. With his horse he dashed into the woods, and soon beheld a hideous beast approaching him. The horse was frightened. He snorted and raised himself

up on his hind legs. St. George spurred him on to attack the fiery-eyed dragon. Opening its jaws, again and again the hissing dragon snapped at the horse. Several times St. George struck the beast on the head with his lance, but the blows did little harm. They only enraged the dragon more and more. The ugly beast rose to its full height, opened its mouth wider than ever, and leaped for the horse's neck. The horse made a quick turn and the dragon fell to the ground. St. George hastened to take advantage of this, and drove his lance through the jaws of the beast, pinning it to the ground.

The story goes that he firmly tied the head of the dragon, and had the brave girl lead it to the city. The people were terrified as the smiling girl led their ugly enemy into their midst. The women ran screaming to their homes. Men pretended not to fear, but their hearts were trembling.

St. George on his handsome white steed followed close behind the dragon. He told the people as he passed that they need have no fear because the true God had given him power over the dragon. He urged them to be converted and baptised. "Believe in the great God Who has given me this victory," he said, "and I shall kill the dragon this day."

God blessed St. George in his fight with the dragon because He wished to make known to the people His great power. The people of the town were soon converted and baptised. They gave rich gifts to St. George, but this true friend of God gave everything to the poor. No greater reward could be given to him than to see the people believe in the God Whom he loved and served, and to see their lives freed not only from the cruel dragon but from the pagan gods whom they had served.

St. George was a brave loyal soldier of his country and a holy faithful soldier of his God.

COPY AND FILL IN THE BLANKS

1. Those are called martyrs who ——.
2. George said to the emperor ——.
3. The emperor was angry when he heard that George ——.
4. The dragon first ate ——; then ——, and finally ——.
5. The last plan of the frantic people was ——.
6. Before fighting with the dragon, George ——.
7. The greatest reward that the people could give George was ——.

XXX

SAINT CLARE

1. IN THE GARDEN

The happy voices of little children could be heard as they ran here and there along the garden paths. Such cheerful faces and happy hearts!

"Where is Clare?" asked a dark-haired girl.

"Clare! Clare!" called the group of girls, seeking their playmate who had disappeared. They knew that Clare was hidden somewhere in that large, lovely garden and they wished to find her. Over the pebble paths they scampered, looking here and there. Now and then they buried their faces in sweet-smelling roses, or drew aside thorny branches to look beyond the leafy bushes.

"Oh! here she is," called out the tallest girl in the party, as she peeked through some large bushes covered with roses. Clare did not know that her hiding place had been discovered. The girls ran quickly to the spot where their com-

panion stood. They, too, looked through the opening in the bushes, and saw Clare kneeling upon the ground with her hands folded in prayer. Before her was a picture of Our Lord and a tiny statue of the Blessed Virgin.

2. A BASKET OF PRAYERS

The girls were surprised. They stood still for a few minutes and watched the holy Clare. They noticed that every little while she would reach to the ground, pick up a small pebble, and place it in a pretty little basket at her side.

The girls dared not make a noise lest they should disturb their pious playmate. They knew that she was praying, but they could not imagine why she was putting the stones in the basket.

One by one, they silently stole away to the other end of the garden. Here beneath an orange tree, they sat whispering till Clare returned to them. She blushed when they told her that they had been watching her. She felt offended at this. She thought that only her dear Lord and the Blessed Mother had heard the sighs of love and the prayers that went forth from her childish heart. But she quickly forgave her friends. One of the girls, who happened to be her sister, said to her, "Why were you counting the stones when you were praying?"

Clare smiled and answered: "My dear sister, I was not counting stones. I was just giving a little basket of prayers to Our Lord. Each stone I placed in the basket represented a prayer. Sometimes I give our Blessed Mother an apronful of prayers. I hope that our dear Lord and His mother are pleased with my gifts."

3. SOLDIERS ATTACK THE CONVENT OF ST. CLARE

Long years afterwards, this same Clare gave up her beautiful home and pretty clothes to become a Sister in a poor convent. Her parents were very angry but they could not make her change her mind. Soon many other pious girls went to live with her and give themselves to God. God loved them and blessed them.

Once a cruel king sent soldiers to attack the town of Assisi. They were to carry away anything of value that they could find. On their way to Assisi, they passed the convent where Saint Clare ,and the other holy Sisters were living. The soldiers decided to break into the convent and steal whatever they could. The walls around the convent were so high that they could not climb over them. They started to build ladders with which to scale the walls.

The terrified Sisters ran to the room of Saint Clare. They knew that she had been sick in bed for some time, but in their fright they went to her for help. "O Sister," they cried, "the soldiers are about to climb the walls. What shall we. do? We have hidden the chalices and the Mass vestments, but they may kill us in their anger. What can we do?"

It seemed foolish for these Sisters to seek aid at the bedside of one who could not walk. But they had not come in vain. She asked the Sisters to carry her on a cot to the gates of the monastery. They looked from one to the other and wondered if Saint Clare had lost her mind. She quietly repeated the request in a voice they had to obey. She then told them to place the monstrance with the Sacred Host in it on a high stand just inside the gates. The Sisters did not know what Saint Clare's plans were, but they were certain that God would help her to carry them out.

4. GOD DEFENDS HIS CHOSEN ONES

The Sisters obeyed, but they obeyed very unwillingly. They thought that the orders of Saint Clare would surely bring death to them and to herself. The cot with the suffering saint was

placed at the gates, near the stand upon which
Our Lord rested in the golden monstrance.

The soldiers had heard the creaking of the
large iron gates as the Sisters slowly opened

them.   They threw aside their nails and ham-
mers and rushed for the gates.   Imagine their
surprise when they saw a sick Sister kneeling in
prayer before the newly made altar!   They stood
dazed for a moment.   The breeze brought echoes
of a prayer to their ears: "O my God, let not
Thy servants fall into the hands of these pagan
soldiers.   Protect them, O God, and protect me."

The soldiers heard the answer from heaven, "I shall always protect you."

A sudden terror struck the hearts of the men. The color left their cheeks as they fled in disorder down the hillside. When the Sisters recovered from their fright and saw what had happened, they fell down in adoration before the throne of Him Who had saved them from death.

COPY AND FILL IN THE BLANKS

1. Clare's companions saw her kneeling in ——.
2. She counted her prayers by ——.
3. When she grew older, Clare became ——.
4. Saint Clare told the Sisters to place —— on a high stand near the gate.
5. Because of Saint Clare's prayers, God saved the Sisters from ——.

XXXI

JESUS REWARDS HIS BELOVED

1. THE SACRAMENT OF LOVE

Long years ago when Jesus lived on this earth, He rejoiced with the happy and He wept with those in sorrow. His heart was filled with love for men. It was because of His great love that He left us Himself in the Blessed Sacrament of the altar. Jesus, Our Lord and Our God, dwells there to be the food of our souls. Before His throne we kneel to pour forth our hearts in love and praise. Forever praised and loved be Jesus in the Holy Sacrament of the altar!

The greatest joy of many saints was to adore Our Lord in the Blessed Sacrament, and to receive Him into their pure hearts. They loved to spend their days and nights in the presence of Jesus, the Prisoner of our altars. Such a holy soul was Saint Catherine of Siena.

Even as a small child, she often set aside

pleasant food and the sweet things of which
children are so fond. For the love of Jesus, she
generally lived on water, wine, and bread. Her
little heart was rapt in thoughts of God.

2. SAINT CATHERINE AFTER RECEIVING HOLY
COMMUNION

Later she wanted to be closer to Jesus, so
she became a Sister. Life in the convent with
the holy friends of God made her happy. Now
she could visit Jesus often during the day and
night.

The other Sisters noticed the beautiful smile
that came upon the face of Saint Catherine as
she knelt in prayer after receiving Holy Communion. A bright heavenly light seemed to
shine from her. Saint Catherine made no short
thanksgivings after Communion like many people
to-day. When she received her God, an endless
stream of prayers went forth from her pure heart.
She adored God, she thanked Him, and she
pleaded with Him for favors and for forgiveness.
She knew that she had her Lord in her heart and

that He was eager to listen to her prayers. Many times she remained bowed in prayer long after the other Sisters had left the chapel.

At these times, Saint Catherine was very happy because she was alone with Jesus. She could now pour out all the love and fervor that lay hidden in her soul. She often cast herself upon the stone floor and told Jesus how her heart burned with love for Him.

3. THE INFANT JESUS APPEARS TO SAINT CATHERINE

Our Lord loved Saint Catherine and showed in more ways than one that she had found favor in His sight. Once she was kneeling in prayer in the simple little chapel of the convent. The Blessed Sacrament was on the altar in a shining gold monstrance. Clouds of sweet-smelling smoke from the incense glided toward the blue ceiling.

Saint Catherine heard the sound of music. She looked at the altar. There, to her surprise, she saw angels holding a beautiful golden veil.

In the middle of the veil was a white Host that took the form of a tiny Infant. It was Jesus in the Sacrament of His love. In her joy, Saint

Catherine cried out, "I believe, O Lord, I believe that You are truly present in the Sacrament of Your love."

4. ANGELS ADORE THE BLESSED SACRAMENT

One night, some months later, Saint Catherine thought that Jesus was lonely in His prison home. The other Sisters had fallen asleep. Not a sound could be heard except the tick, tick of the hall clock. Saint Catherine quietly tiptoed down the narrow hall, fearful lest she might disturb the sleep of the tired Sisters. As she entered the dark chapel, she saw the tiny red light flickering before the altar to remind us that Jesus is there.

Saint Catherine knelt at her usual place to keep Jesus company. With a heart filled with love, she spoke to her Lord: "O dear Jesus, how forgetful the world is toward You! Night after night, You dwell on lonely altars with no one to worship or to love You."

She was suddenly startled from her prayer by a flood of golden light that appeared around the altar. There she saw a wonderful sight. Bright angels and white-robed saints bowed low in adoration before Jesus in the Blessed Sacrament, singing hymns of praise and glory to God, our King. Catherine bowed her head too, and silently joined in the beautiful song, her heart overflowing with happiness.

5. AT THE ALTAR RAIL

On another occasion God rewarded Saint Catherine for her devotion to the Blessed Sacrament. One morning, she was attending Mass in the chapel. When the time arrived for the

people to receive Holy Communion, Saint Catherine, with hands clasped upon her breast, approached the altar. The priest turned to the people, holding the Sacred Host in his hand. In a low voice he said: "O Lord, I am not worthy that You should come to me. Say but the word and my soul shall be healed." Three times that prayer was brought by the angels to the throne of God in heaven.

The priest then glanced at the altar rail. He saw Saint Catherine kneeling there, a circle of light about her. Overcome with emotion, he said to the Sacred Host in his hand: "Go, O Lord. Go and find Your beloved." Perhaps he thought himself unworthy to place the Host on the tongue of the Lord's chosen friend. As soon as he spoke, the Host left his hands, and flew to the tongue of Saint Catherine.

6. THE LOST HOST

The holy Sister Catherine had been ill. She was advised by the other Sisters not to go into the church nor to try to receive Holy Communion. But when no one was near, she dressed herself and went to the church, hoping to hear Mass.

The hour was late, but a pious old priest was just beginning Mass. Saint Catherine went to the back of the church. How eager she was to

receive Holy Communion! Oh, if her dear Lord would only come to her! She knelt sadly in the dark corner, and told Jesus how anxious she was to welcome Him into her heart.

The priest continued his Mass, never knowing that God's holy friend was praying in the church. The time came for him to separate the Host into two parts. To his surprise, it divided into three parts. The priest went on with the Mass. He struck his breast three times, and begged

God for mercy for sinners. The communion prayers were then said. When the priest began to place the pieces of the Sacred Host between his fingers, he noticed that one of the pieces had disappeared. He looked around on the altar and on the floor, but no trace of it could be found. He finished the Mass, and later returned to the altar to look for the lost portion of the Sacred Host. It could be seen nowhere.

Excited and worried, he went to the pastor and told him what had happened. Both then hurried back to the church, but their search for the Host was in vain. Then a thought came to the mind of the gray-haired pastor. "Perhaps Sister Catherine was in the church and received that Host," he said. But the other priest insisted that he had seen no one in the church.

They went to the convent where they met Saint Catherine. She admitted that she had been in the church during the Mass. Then they told her the story of the missing Host. She said that they had no reason to worry, because God would take care of it. This answer did not satisfy the priests. Finally Saint Catherine told them that Jesus Himself had brought to her the piece of the Sacred Host that was supposed to have been lost.

How happy Saint Catherine must have been in her love for Jesus in the Blessed Sacrament! Her heart could never thank God enough for the wonderful ways in which He rewarded her for her devotion to Him in the Sacrament of His love.

Do we love Jesus in the Blessed Sacrament as Saint Catherine did? I wonder if we really love to receive Him often into our little hearts. Perhaps sometimes we forget to thank Him for coming to us in Holy Communion. Saint Catherine knew that the time after Communion is very precious, for it is then that we truly carry Jesus in our hearts. God favored Saint Catherine because she loved Him. He will favor us if we love Him.

The best way that we can show our love for Jesus is to keep His Commandments and receive Him often in Holy Communion.

ANSWER THESE QUESTIONS

1. Why does God remain with us in the Blessed Sacrament?

2. Why did Saint Catherine enter the convent?

3. What did Saint Catherine do after receiving Holy Communion?

4. What lesson should we learn from this?

5. Our Lord showed several times how much He loved to be with Saint Catherine.   Tell the story of one of these events.

XXXII

SAINT FRANCIS AND BROTHER WOLF

1. THE BLACK WOLF OF GUBBIO

Up among the beautiful hills of northern Italy lies the quaint old town of Gubbio, with its narrow crooked streets and its gayly-colored houses. Hundreds of years ago, in the days of Saint Francis of Assisi, the little town was one of the most talked-about places in the country. This was because of a strange, unwelcome visitor that often found his way into the town. The visitor was a large black wolf.

This wolf was not satisfied with stealing lambs and carrying them to his den in the forest. From time to time, he prowled about the woods seeking for children who went there to play. The people became alarmed and warned the children not to go to the woods any more.

The wolf wondered what was the matter. He

was finding no more little boys for his dinner. For many days, he lay in wait near the entrance to the woods, but nobody came to pick pretty flowers or to play hide-and-seek. The hungry wolf was disappointed. He wondered what he would do.

At last he said to himself, "I am strong and brave. All the men in the town fear me. When I howl and snarl, they tremble. I shall sneak into the town at evening and snatch any child I find." So later on, when the shadows of night were falling, the wolf slyly made his way into the town. He crept along the wall of the old church, and hid himself in its shadows.

2. NIGHTLY VISITS

Soon he heard the joyful voices of little children as they laughed and sang at play. He opened his mouth and licked his lips. He crouched farther back in the corner. The children were coming nearer and nearer. They were now but a short distance away. It was the kind old priest of the town and a group of little children playing about him. The wolf thought to himself, "That little boy who toddles along with his brother will be my dinner tonight."

As soon as the happy gathering passed by, the wolf sprang from his hiding place. He

snatched the little boy and dashed for the woods. The children screamed, and the aged priest ran down the street crying: "Wolf! Wolf! The wolf has taken a boy."

Men rushed from their homes with clubs and swords. They hastened down the street, but the wolf had disappeared in the darkness. In vain they searched the woods with lanterns. No trace of the boy or the wolf could be found.

Time and again, the wolf repeated his visit to the city and returned to his cave with a lamb or a little child. The poor people became frantic. No man would dare fight the wolf single-handed. His very name brought terror to their hearts. So daring had the wolf become, that even in daylight he prowled around near the town. The fear of him was so great that men no longer traveled alone beyond the city. They went in groups armed with swords and strong clubs. Day after day, morning, noon, and night, the frightened people spoke about their terrible visitor from the forest. In every home, little children gathered about their mothers' knees in the evening and prayed God to save them from the wolf of Gubbio.

3. SAINT FRANCIS VISITS THE WOLF

It was during all this excitement that Saint Francis visited the city to preach to the people. He soon found out that the people were more anxious to tell him about their enemy than to listen to his sermons. Saint Francis pitied the poor people. His loving heart overflowed with sympathy as they told him about their dear little ones who had been taken by the fierce wolf.

Saint Francis said to them, "I shall visit Brother Wolf and see what I can do with him." The men and women warned him not to go near the savage beast, but no fear entered Francis' heart. His disciples and some of the people started out with him to find the wolf's den in the woods. But they were all afraid to follow too closely. They remained some distance behind, as Francis, trusting in God, went forward to the place where the wolf lay.

When the wolf saw the crowd of people, he sprang to his feet, and, with open mouth, came snarling forth to attack Francis. The people shuddered. Women screamed and ran back toward the town. Only Saint Francis remained calm. He made the sign of the cross, and called the wolf to him saying: "Come here, Brother Wolf. I command you in the name of Jesus

Christ that you do no harm to me nor to any other man."

4. THE WOLF IS TAMED

At the voice of Francis, the growling beast closed his mouth, lowered his head, and, meek

as a lamb, walked to the feet of the saint. He sat down like a pet dog and looked into the kind face of the holy man from Assisi. The people were astonished. Could this be the wolf of Gubbio? Could this be the savage animal that had filled their hearts with fear?

Saint Francis again spoke to the wolf, saying: "Brother Wolf, you have done a great deal of harm in this neighborhood. Not only have you killed and eaten the gentle lambs of the field, but you have also dared to take little children. For these things, you should have been put to death. Daily the poor, frightened people cry out against you. But I wish to make peace between you and them, that you may harm them no more, and that they may forgive your terrible crimes of the past." The wolf wagged its tail, bowed its head, and tried to look kindly into the face of Saint Francis. He did all these things to show that he agreed with what the saint was saying.

The people were now more surprised than before. The wolf showed that he understood what Francis was talking about.

The saint then continued: "Because you are glad to make this peace, I promise you that the people of the town will feed you as long as you live. But I also want you to promise me that you will never harm a lamb or a child again. Do you promise?"

The wolf again bowed his head, and thus gave a sign that he made the promise.

Saint Francis stretched forth his hand as a pledge of his faith, and the wolf placed his right paw in the hand. Saint Francis patted the head of the wolf and said: "Brother Wolf, I command you to follow me, and we shall go forth and conclude this peace in God's name."

5. AT THE MARKET-PLACE

Back into the city, Saint Francis went, and the wolf of Gubbio followed him as meekly as a lamb. The story of how Saint Francis had tamed the wolf reached the city before him. Men, women, and children gathered in the streets to see the holy man and their old-time enemy. The look on Saint Francis' face showed the people that it was no time for shouting or cheering. They blessed themselves, and thanked God for this wonderful miracle, as the saint and the wolf slowly walked through the streets to the market place.

Here large crowds had gathered. They were

now eager to listen to what the holy man from
Assisi had to say. Saint Francis stood upon
a stone near the drinking fountain and preached
to the people saying: "God has permitted evil
things to come upon you to punish you for your

sins. You have feared the wrath of this wolf,
but far more dangerous are the flames of hell
that last forever. When the jaws of one small
animal can terrify and alarm you, how much
more should you fear the jaws of hell? Therefore, turn away from your sinful lives, and God

will save you from the jaws of the wolf now and from the fires of hell in the time to come."

Saint Francis then told the people about the agreement he had made with the wolf. From then on. the wolf meekly went from door to door, eating the food that the people were glad to give him.

ARE THESE TRUE OR FALSE?

1. Gubbio was the home of a wicked wolf.
2. The wolf was glad when no boys came to the woods.
3. Men hastened after the wolf with clubs and swords.
4. After his first visit to the city, the wolf was afraid to return.
5. Saint Francis went to Gubbio because he had heard about the wolf.
6. Francis trembled when the wolf came near him.
7. The wolf barked to show that he agreed with Francis.
8. The jaws of hell are more terrible than the jaws of the wolf.

XXXIII

IMELDA

1. IMELDA LOVES TO LEARN ABOUT JESUS

Imelda was a sweet, delicate child with the face of an angel. Nothing pleased her better than to hear her nurse or her mother speak about our dear Lord and His friends. Indeed, she sometimes complained that her nurse did not tell her enough about God.

The little heart of Imelda was always glad when someone read to her from the Bible about God. She listened carefully and often asked questions. In fact, she asked so many questions that her mother and the nurse could not answer them all. At times she seemed to know more about God than they did.

Whenever anything was read about Holy Communion, little Imelda was very interested. She wanted to know all about this wonderful gift that Our Lord has given to us. She often asked her mother to read over again the stories about Jesus and Holy Communion. Then she would ask question after question. The pious mother blushed with shame when she could not answer the questions of her little child.

One evening, after Imelda had gone to sleep, her parents spoke about her interest in learning all she could about God. They felt that they did not know enough to teach her. So it was decided to have one of the Sisters in the convent teach their little daughter about God and His kingdom.

2. STUDYING AT THE CONVENT

The Sister Superior was glad to appoint one of the nuns to teach the little Imelda. So every day the eager child hurried to the convent to listen to the Sister's lessons about God. That was the happiest time of the day for her. She never grew tired of learning her catechism. It was her most interesting lesson, for she dearly loved the Lord Jesus. Do we love God as Imelda did? I wonder if we are as anxious to learn all about Him as she was.

When the Sister spoke lovingly about the birth of the Infant Jesus in the cold, damp cave, teardrops rolled down the cheeks of the child as she thought to herself, "Oh! If I could only have given Him my beautiful crib or my pretty pink blanket!"

The eyes of Imelda danced with delight whenever the Sister showed her the picture of Our Lord blessing the little children. She liked to imagine herself one of the happy children that played about the Savior. Her joy was complete when the Sister asked her to whisper what she thought each child was saying to Jesus. Her sweet soul would give forth a shower of fervent prayers of love.

The pitiful story of the suffering and death of Jesus was too much for her loving heart. Time and again, with eyes filled with tears, she would ask, "Oh! Why were they so cruel to dear Jesus?"

The good Sister could now teach her many

things about Holy Communion that her mother did not know. She explained first how Our Lord promised to give His Body and Blood to us. Then she told the story of the Last Supper, showing Imelda a beautiful picture of Our Lord and the apostles gathered around the table. The little child let no word escape her.

When the Sister had finished, Imelda could tell the story of how Our Lord the night before He died, took bread, and blessed and broke it. Then He gave it to His disciples, as He said, "Take ye and eat. This is My Body." He next took the chalice. He gave thanks, and passed it to them saying: "Drink ye all of this, for this is My Blood of the New Testament which shall be shed for many unto the remission of sins."

The Sister taught her little friend about God's great love for us that makes Him hide all His power and glory under a tiny Host.

"And is God really and truly in the tiny Host?" Imelda asked one day.

"Yes, He is just as really in the Host as He

was when He sat near the well and blessed the little children," the Sister answered.

"Well, then, the church is truly God's house, because Jesus is really there," she exclaimed.

Her joy would know no limit when the nun spoke about Jesus and the Blessed Sacrament. She longed to kneel before Him and whisper prayers of tender love and devotion from her pure heart. Often when her playmates were enjoying their games, Imelda would steal away to the convent church to talk to Jesus. Her childish heart knew no fear. It was all love — love for Jesus.

Imelda often asked her teacher when Jesus would come to her. Oh, how she longed to receive Him and hold Him in her breast! But alas! in those days children did not receive Holy Communion until they were fourteen years of age. So Imelda had to wait. How happy we should be that we can receive our dear Lord every day if we wish to! It makes Jesus happy too when He sees little boys and girls welcome Him daily in their hearts.

3. SISTER IMELDA

The little girl desired to be as near the Lord as possible. She was a mere child, yet she wanted to live in the house where Jesus lived. One day she spoke to her parents about joining the Sisters in the convent. They were happy at the thought, but they told her she must wait for a time, because she was so young. For Imelda, however, there was to be no waiting. She pleaded again and again, and her parents finally gave their consent.

In the convent, the pious child was happier than ever. She was near Jesus and daily helped one of the Sisters clean and decorate His altar. How proud she felt when she gathered pretty flowers in the garden for the altar of dear Jesus! Her days were one long prayer of joy.

Soon she was given a lovely white robe like the other Sisters wore. She was now permitted to pray with them in the chapel and to sing the praises of God.

When the other Sisters received Holy Communion, Imelda knelt in her place, praying God to hasten the day when she might join them.

She watched the holy joy that lit up their faces as they brought Jesus back from the altar with them.

There was one thing that Imelda could never understand about Holy Communion. She wondered how anyone could receive Holy Communion and not die of joy. The good Sisters tried to give her an answer, but the answer never satisfied her. Again and again, she brought up this question in talking with the Sisters. She thought that the soul must burst with joy when it received Jesus.

4. HER FIRST AND LAST COMMUNION

One morning, Imelda knelt in the chapel rapt in prayer, while the other Sisters, one by one, went to the altar to receive Holy Communion. Her little heart burned with a desire to welcome Jesus into her soul. She buried her face in her hands, and poured out her soul to God. She pleaded with her God to come to her.

"O Lord I am not worthy that You should come to me, but only say the word and my soul will be healed." Over and over again with tender devotion, she sent her message to God, "Sweet Jesus, I cannot go to You, so won't You come to me?"

The child was roused from her prayer by a bright light that appeared near the altar. It began to move nearer and nearer to her. In the golden light, she noticed the tiny Host. The other Sisters saw the light and fell upon their knees in amazement. The light and the Host came to the place where Imelda was praying.

Now more fervently than ever she prayed, "O Lord I am not worthy. Say but the word and my soul will be healed."

There in the air the Host remained, until the priest came and placed it upon the tongue of the happy girl. She bowed her head in prayer. The other Sisters quietly left the chapel while Imelda welcomed her God.

After some time, the Sister Superior sent one of the Sisters to tell Imelda to come for her breakfast. The Sister approached the kneeling form and called, "Imelda! Imelda!" But there was no response. Then she stepped closer and touched the child's arm. Imelda did not move. Imelda was dead! She had received her God, and died of joy.

ANSWER THESE QUESTIONS

1. As a small child, how did Imelda show her love for God?

2. Of all the lessons she studied, which did she like best?

3. Why did she want to live in the convent?

4. What was her one great wish?

5. What could she not understand about Holy Communion?

6. How did Our Lord answer her prayer?

CPSIA information can be obtained
at www.ICGtesting.com
Printed in the USA
FFHW021642280119
50263054-55264FF